Greater Than the Sum of Our Parts

"Precisely the book our movements need and deserve. Crafted from decades of transnational activism and based on radical intellectual traditions, Nada Elia brilliantly weaves together the challenges of our time and the political frameworks necessary to overcome them."

—Noura Erakat, Associate Professor,
Rutgers University–New Brunswick

"Nada Elia's *Greater Than the Sum of Our Parts* is an inspiring call to action that deconstructs the many oppressive systems we currently find ourselves struggling against, and shows us the way forward."

—Adam Horowitz, Executive Editor, *Mondoweiss*

"I am so grateful that a book such as *Greater Than the Sum of Our Parts* finally exists! Reading it felt like drinking cold water on a parched day. The writing is bold and brave, the analysis clear-sighted and unflinching. And yet somehow, on top of all this, the book is full of heart, fierce love and radical empathy. A must read."

—Jen Marlowe, author of *I Am Troy Davis* and *The Hour of Sunlight*

"In *Greater Than the Sum of Our Parts*, author and long-time activist for Palestinian liberation Nada Elia makes a compelling, even irresistible, case for moving beyond rights and statehood for Palestine to a truly decolonial future. Grounded in the analysis of actual struggles, the book is informed by her commitment to abolitionist feminist practice, which reorients the vision of what a post-Zionist Palestine could look like in crucial ways. Defined by solidarity rather than exceptionalism, this is a truly necessary book."

—David Lloyd, Department of English, University of California, Riverside

"Nada Elia offers a new map altogether: a map of survival, possibility, and hope. Like the Palestinian struggle for freedom itself, this map is collective, collaborative, built on and for radical love."

—Sherene Seikaly, Associate Professor, Department of History, University of California, Santa Barbara

Greater Than the Sum of Our Parts

Feminism, Inter/Nationalism, and Palestine

Nada Elia

First published 2023 by Pluto Press
New Wing, Somerset House, Strand, London WC2R 1LA
and Pluto Press Inc.
1930 Village Center Circle, 3-834, Las Vegas, NV 89134

www.plutobooks.com

British Library Cataloguing in Publication Data
A catalogue record for this book is available from the British Library

ISBN   978 0 7453 4747 9   Paperback
ISBN   978 0 7453 4750 9   PDF
ISBN   978 0 7453 4749 3   EPUB

This book is printed on paper suitable for recycling and made from fully managed
and sustained forest sources. Logging, pulping and manufacturing processes are
expected to conform to the environmental standards of the country of origin.

Typeset by Stanford DTP Services, Northampton, England

Simultaneously printed in the United Kingdom and United States of America

To the young, who never forgot

Contents

Preface: Crevices of Hope

As I write this, fires are burning everywhere. Climate catastrophes, in the form of droughts, floods, heat waves, and ravaging flames, are the new normal, even as the communities most impacted by these disasters remain utterly vulnerable, with inadequate resources and nowhere to run to. Journeys to safer places, whether on small crafts ill-equipped to face hungry ocean waves, or in unventilated trucks in the scorching desert heat, prove deadly. If and when they reach a border, the refugees are unwelcome, subjected to even more violence: prison, slave labor, and deportation. Palestinian refugees, on the other hand, organize return marches to their own towns and villages, only to be shot at by the Israeli occupation forces. In the unsurpassed words of Warsan Shire: "You only leave home when home won't let you stay."[1]

The exceptional welcome afforded Ukrainian refugees while other equally desperate people are refused entry confirms that racism is at the very heart of Global North xenophobia. What we are witnessing, at the borders, is the equivalent of the worst days of apartheid, slavery, and Jim Crow laws. The "Whites Only" signs, temporarily stashed away, might as well be polished off and placed on full display again.

Systemic racism, like misogyny and homophobia, is a manifestation of state violence, which seems relentless. In the USA, there is currently a national debate about the ethics of allowing a ten-year-old girl to end a pregnancy resulting from rape. Let me restate that: a ten-year-old girl was raped. The recent decision of the Supreme Court of the United States has made it so that the state she lives in, Ohio, does not allow her to abort past six weeks' gestation, even though her pregnancy is the result of rape and she may die in labor. Americans need not look to the Taliban for crimes against womanhood; we have our own version here in the USA, where an "originalist" Supreme Court still seeks guidance from a document penned over two centuries ago by the founders of a settler colonial country that sought to exterminate the Indigenous people of the continent it was stealing, while relying on the labor of enslaved Africans. Many of those "founding fathers" had no qualms raping young girls themselves, so as to "father," but certainly not parent, children who would increase their wealth as slaveowners.

The ruthless violence of racist settler colonialism is also on full display throughout Palestine. Israeli settlers continue to attack Palestinian towns, as in Masafer Yatta, and Palestinian homes as in Jerusalem, while Israeli soldiers continue to raze villages such as al-Araqeeb, raid cities such as Jenin, and bomb refugees in the blockaded Gaza Strip. Diaspora Palestinians such as myself are turned away at the airport if we attempt to visit our own country. If the Israeli Occupation Forces are the world's most moral army, I'll take "immorality": young children hurling rocks at tanks. That gesture, whether by children or grown women or men, captures our defiance and our irrepressible urge to live in dignity.[2]

But this is not a book about the repulsiveness of militarism, racism, and intolerance of difference that seem to fuel today's crimes. Seventy-five years after the onset of al-Nakba, there is no avoiding a discussion of the evils committed over the decades since Israel was founded on the ruins of our homes. Nor will I shy away from discussing the murderous misogyny and homophobia poisoning our own communities, as we struggle to overcome the ravages of dispossession. Still, I do not want this book to be one more analysis of the many forms of the suffering we have endured. Despite my realism about the horrors all around us, this is a hopeful book.

The pressure from above seems unforgiving. And yes, we are cracking under it. In addition to the multifaceted violence of settler colonialism and apartheid, our communities are experiencing increased violence perpetrated by Palestinians against Palestinians, the inevitable trickling down of macro-oppression into the domestic sphere. Homophobia, domestic violence, and femicides are on the rise. Fathers are killing their daughters, and influential writers are accusing queers of placing "the gay agenda" above the national struggle—as if queers were not part of the nation, and do not want liberation. Such are the consequences of imperial feminism, which presents women's rights as a Western gift to the benighted Orient, and of pinkwashing, which celebrates Israel as gay-friendly, because its soldiers can fly a Pride flag after torturing Palestinian prisoners.

Freedom for only some is not freedom at all. It is merely privilege if it does not also extend to the most marginalized members of our societies. But there is light breaking through the fragmentation. New life is germinating in the crevices of hope. Just as, globally, from the USA to Israel, structural oppression stems from the same systems: capitalism, neoliberalism, "development," and militarized right-wing authoritarianism, so resistance worldwide is grounded in similar impulses toward liberation—a global intifada from Turtle Island to Palestine. Displaced, diasporic, dispossessed, we are coming together. We are survivors, and we partake of and share the bounty of a radical love that cannot be stolen from us. The Red Nation, a coalition of Indigenous organizers committed to Native liberation, wants to abolish borders and welcome relatives from around the world, while declaring that: "Palestine is the moral barometer of Indigenous North America."[3] We are sustained within our chosen families; we support each other, knowing our strength lies in our deep connections. Mi casita es su casita. Visit Palestine, where you can soak in our *sumoud*, the irrepressible determination to live freely, in dignity, undaunted by the might of the Israel–Global North alliance. This is why Israeli soldiers in armored tanks are scared of our barefoot children: we remain defiant.

And as old concepts of identity are eroding, we are forming new coalitions. Where once we identified primarily as Palestinian, Black, Navajo, Kanaka Maoli, men, women, straight, or lesbian, we now also view ourselves as decolonial, feminist, Indigenous, non-binary, queer. Our communities are like seismic plates shifting and forming new blocs—a mosaic made up of the many shards of our identities, glued together by the sweat and blood of our protesting, rebelling, dreaming, scheming, and organizing together, across the arbitrary borders that fail to contain us.

It is beautiful, and fluid.

This is what liberation looks like.

This is the global intifada that this book explores and celebrates. I have written about it in a style that I hope is accessible to all, shying away, as much as possible, from jargon and academic obfuscation. My intent is to express, not to impress. To invite, to welcome, rather than intimidate. We, the survivors, buoy each other. Separately, we endure, persist, stay alive. Together, we overcome and thrive.

Finally, I trust it is understood that no book on social movements is the work of its author alone. Mine is no exception. The activists and organizers who made this book possible are too many to list here. I am fortunate enough to be friends with many of them, while others are role models, inspirations, or the youth I want to be when I grow up. I would be remiss, however, if I did not name the close friends who were directly or indirectly involved in it, by reading chapters, discussing ideas, sustaining me, or offering me a place to stay and write: Yamila Channan, Nadine Naber, Jen Marlowe, Sherene Seikaly, Art Vertner, and my many sisters and queer kin in the Palestinian Feminist Collective.

Introduction:
Feminist, Abolitionist, and Indigenous Horizons in the Struggle Against Settler Colonialism and Apartheid

The most iconic representation of the Palestinian people today, as it has been for decades, is that of the young Handala. a ten-year-old refugee boy in tattered clothes, disheveled, barefoot, his back turned to the world. Handala was created in 1969 by Palestinian political cartoonist Naji al-Ali, who had himself become a refugee in 1948 at the age of ten. The young character is generally viewed as a symbol of defiance, persistence, and a reminder of the Right of Return. His creator, however, explained that he named him Handala after the very bitter gourd fruit native to the land of Palestine. To be a refugee is, first and foremost, a bitter experience.

And the most significant symbol of the Palestinian condition is the brass skeleton house key—a physical memento of the homes Palestinians left behind in 1947 and 1948 as they were forcibly expelled, or fled in fear for their lives, and which they fully expected to return to in a matter of weeks, once the fighting had subsided. Three quarters of a century later, many Palestinian families still hold on to that key, passed down through the generations of refugee life. Some are a mere few miles away from their homes, others, halfway around the globe.

A peaceful people living in dignity on their land who, for reasons beyond their control or understanding, were attacked and occupied by foreign forces (Great Britain) which enabled foreign colonial

1

settlers (Zionists) to expel them, destroy their villages and claim their property as their own, and eventually establish Israel in Palestine. This is the essence of the story of my family and my people,

writes Samir Abed-Rabbo, author of *One Democratic State*.[1] My own mother, a teenager when she fled her homeland in 1948, was among those dispossessed by the newly established settler colonial state, which never allowed her to return. She married my father, like her a Palestinian refugee from Jerusalem, in Iraq, and gave birth to her four children in two different diaspora countries. My mother was widowed in 1967, becoming the single parent of four girls, my sisters and me, the oldest of whom was not yet ten years old. Her struggles, *our* struggles as exiled Palestinian women, while sadly all too common, are rarely centered in mainstream discussions of Palestinian resistance, which is instead generally understood in masculinist militarized terms. And yet, in the streets and the fields, at home and in exile, Palestinian women have resisted, organized, and persisted, even as they faced the multiple challenges of negotiating a patriarchy aggravated by the gendered violence of settler colonialism. From Deir Yassin in 1948, to Sheikh Jarrah in 2021, Palestinian women have put their bodies on the line, and borne the brunt of colonial violence, as they sought to halt the ethnic cleansing of their people. Today, Palestinian women in the homeland continue to be at the forefront of the struggle to defend their homes and their lands, as settlers push them aside, drag them by their scarves, and brutalize them in the violent quest to transform Palestine into the Jewish state. In the diaspora, Palestinian women are also at the forefront of organizing, from the grassroots to academia to the legal field, as well as in the alternative and mainstream media. The resilience, creativity, defiance, and nurturing love of Handala's many sisters would make Naji al-Ali proud.

Palestine has been battered by over a century of imperialism, its Indigenous people ravaged throughout their historic homeland. Zionists would argue that Palestine "never existed" because it was never a nation state modeled upon the nineteenth-century European concept of countries. This is a manifestation of the same Eurocentric colonial mindset that viewed Turtle Island as vacant land, because the Indigenous nations in what is now known as North America did not have structures recognizable as "national" to the colonizers. It is true that, like much of the region, Palestine had once been part of the Ottoman Empire, before the empire's collapse during World War One. Historians, however, agree that the four centuries of Ottoman rule can generally be characterized as peaceful, as the Ottoman Empire granted subject communities significant autonomy. This changed drastically under the British Mandate, with Britain's cursory dismissal of the Palestinian people's deep attachment to their land. Indeed, the "Arab" Revolt of 1936–1939 was in every way a nationalist, *Palestinian* revolt against Britain's imperial claims to determine the fate of Palestine, and to change parts of it into a "Jewish national home," as stated in a letter from Britain's Foreign Secretary, Arthur Balfour, to Lord Lionel Walter Rothschild, a leader of the British Jewish community. I am referring, of course, to the infamous "Balfour Declaration" of November 1917, a mere sixty-nine words that changed the fate of the region.[2]

In *Culture and Imperialism*, Edward Said argues that imperialism is the ideology, colonialism its on-the-ground manifestation.[3] This ideology, which in Palestine took the form of a cavalier decision, by a foreign power, to create a new country over parts of a pre-existing one, is at the root of today's struggle. Yet, much of the recent analysis of the plight of the Palestinian people focuses on the current system of legalized apartheid that is crushing them. Such analysis is necessary, especially because "apartheid" is internationally recognized as a crime against humanity, whereas settler colonialism is not.[4] And this book is indeed grounded partly in the premise of Israeli apartheid.[5] I do not question this, and appreciate the fact that the case has been successfully expounded on by others, and amply documented by such widely respected human rights monitoring organizations as Human Rights Watch, which in April 2021 issued a 224-page report concluding that Israel is no longer approaching apartheid, but had already resolutely crossed that threshold to become an apartheid regime.[6] Only months earlier, in January 2021, the Israeli human rights monitoring organization B'Tselem had also published a report squarely charging Israel with this crime.[7] And on February 1,

2022, Amnesty International became the third non-Palestinian human rights organization to accuse Israel of practicing apartheid in its own 280-page report, "Israel's Apartheid Against Palestinians: Cruel System of Domination and Crime Against Humanity."[8] Palestinians, of course, had long stated that Israel's state-sanctioned Jewish supremacy amounts to apartheid, and the 2005 call for Boycott, Divestment, and Sanctions (BDS) on Israel until it abides by international law makes it clear that the campaign is inspired by the South African anti-apartheid struggle, precisely because the Boycott National Committee, the organizing body behind the BDS call, believed Israel was committing this crime.

While it is sobering to note that an accusation against Israel carries more weight when made by anyone other than the Palestinians, I am not interested in merely adding to the chorus of arguments that "it is apartheid." Instead, I elaborate on both the similarities and the differences between the Israeli and South African systems, to better address the accusation that critics of Israel are unfairly singling out that country for opprobrium. As I will show in Chapter 2, "Déjà Vu: Beyond Apartheid," apologists of South Africa's apartheid regime also protested that that country was being singled out for criticism. The comparison also helps in offering critical insights from last century's struggle to overthrow South Africa's apartheid, that can hopefully guide this century's organizing for justice for Palestine. My focus is on the *effects* of oppression, and on the current struggles to overcome the oppressive system, rather than on that system itself. As I compare and contrast, I pay particular attention to women's circumstances, as settler colonialism and racism are always gendered, and have historically brought gendered manifestations of violence. This is evidenced in the rape and murder of Indigenous and Black women in North America, the forced sterilization of women of color in the USA and Israel, and of course Israel's denial of the reproductive rights of Palestinian women. I discuss these, as well as Israel's violence against gender non-conforming Palestinians, throughout this book.

I am also concerned with learning from the shortcomings of the South African struggle, which resulted in overthrowing legalized white supremacy, but not in achieving a fully liberated society. Palestine should be exemplary of more than *sumoud*—our now legendary steadfastness; Palestine should model the new society that abolitionists aspire to, as they look beyond the end of oppression, to life-affirming practices. Sadly, such a concern was not sufficiently foregrounded in the national liberation struggles of the twentieth century, hence the social inequality that plagues postcolonial countries today. But it is very much at the forefront of decolonial praxis today.

The focus on exposing Israel's apartheid rule, one more recently promulgated primarily by non-Palestinians, has facilitated a much-needed global discussion of Israel's discriminatory practices. But the Palestinian people are as much defined by life under settler colonialism, a brutal military occupation, ethnic cleansing, forced exile, and permanent refugee status, as they are by state-sanctioned racism.[9] Thus, I argue that the exclusive focus on apartheid, evidenced in some of the recent titles about Palestine,[10] as well as the Human Rights Watch and B'Tselem reports, is insufficient for a formulation of the solution to the plight of the Palestinians as a colonized, displaced, and majority-refugee people, even if it proves useful in exposing Israel's crimes, and debunking the young country's claim to be a democracy.

Most Palestinians identify primarily as a people who have lost their homeland, and continue to lose their homes and lands. Apartheid, a system of legalized racism, is a logical progeny of imperialist ideology, and of that ideology's on-the-ground manifestation, colonialism. It is one of the many weapons of imperialism. Simply put, there would be no apartheid in Palestine if it were not for settler colonialism. It is therefore time to reaffirm and emphasize Palestine's reality as a colonized country, whose Indigenous people have been dispossessed and disenfranchised, while settlers, protected by the army, police forces, and legal system of a colonial state, took over, and continue to steal Palestinian lands, homes, villages, and natural resources. Al-Nakba, Arabic for "the catastrophe," is not a historical moment that happened and concluded in May 1948—it is ongoing. Israel's ethnic cleansing of the Palestinians has never stopped; every new settlement is built through the displacement, dispossession, and, often, the murder of Palestinians—a settler colonial move best described by Patrick Wolfe as "the elimination of the native."[11] Settler colonialism "destroys to replace," Wolfe wrote, before quoting Theodor Herzl, the founder of Zionism, as writing in *Der Judenstaat*: "If I wish to substitute a new building for an old one, I must demolish before I construct."[12]

An analysis of settler colonialism, alongside that of apartheid, is imperative. And a reminder of what Abed-Rabbo terms the "essence" of the Palestinian story—namely, the dispossession of a peaceful Indigenous people attacked and occupied by foreign forces—is also necessary, because a discussion of apartheid as the primary form of oppression does not fully address the circumstances of the 2 million Palestinians in the besieged Gaza Strip, over 70 percent of whom are refugees from other parts of historic Palestine. The January 2021 B'Tselem report naming Israel's control of all of historic Palestine as an apartheid regime, while notable for its denunciation of Israel's full control over the entire land "from the river to the sea," including the Gaza Strip, fails to foreground the basic yet significant fact that the majority of Palestinians in that strip are refugees. Titled "A Regime of Jewish Supremacy from the Jordan River to the Mediterranean Sea: This is Apartheid," the B'Tselem report rightly observes that Israel has control over 14 million people, roughly half of them Jewish, and the other half Palestinian, and practices a system of Jewish supremacy throughout historic Palestine. However, when discussing the Gaza Strip, it simply notes that it is "home to about two million Palestinians, also denied political rights," but not that the majority of these Palestinians are displaced from homes and lands and villages and cities that are now part of the Israeli state. It does not note that hunger, like poverty, is feminized, and that a 2017 survey found that 25 percent of pregnant women in Gaza are anemic, and 25 percent of Palestinian women in the Gaza Strip and West Bank are at risk of death during childbirth.[13] And it fails to mention the circumstances of the millions of diaspora Palestinians, who are also subject to Israel's control of Palestine's borders, which impacts their Right of Return.

Meanwhile, the Human Rights Watch report accusing Israel of having crossed the threshold into apartheid fails to discuss the specific gendered aspects of oppression that Palestinian women experience under Israel's control. These include, among numerous other instances, sexual torture in prison, and the widely documented denial of access to hospitals during labor. They also include, for example, a military advisor, Mordechai Kedar, suggesting that Israeli soldiers should rape the mothers and sisters of militant Palestinian men,[14] and a justice minister, Ayelet Shaked, calling for the murder of Palestinian women because they "raise little snakes."[15] The omission of a discussion of Israel's gendered violence in the 2021 Human Rights Watch report is particularly jarring, considering the organization had issued a 105-page report in 2006 looking specifically at violence against Palestinian women and girls in the "Occupied Territories" by family members and intimate partners, while ignoring the many gendered aspects of Israel's state violence.[16] (I use quotation marks around Occupied Territories to tease out the flawed, imperial assumption that the rest of Palestine is not occupied.)

Additionally, the recent widespread currency of the term Gazans, as if they were not first and foremost Palestinians is a double-edged development. It brings attention to their unique circumstances even as it discursively separates them from the rest of their country—thus further contributing to the fragmentation of the Palestinian people. Since the withdrawal of Israeli settlers in 2005, Gaza, as Palestinian geographer Nour Joudah writes, has been "a settler-colonial city without the settlers," and she urges us to look at the Gaza Strip as a model of Indigenous survival, rather than disappearance.[17] Indeed, the innovations coming out of the Gaza Strip, from setting up parkour courses in the apocalyptic landscape of a shell-shocked city, to creating building bricks out of the ash and rubble of bombed out houses, are exemplary of the determination and hopeful ingenuity needed everywhere today. That survival is in large part the result of women's creativeness, organizing, activism, and overall life-affirming practices.

It is important, then, as we explore the solution to the plight of Palestine and the Palestinian people, to discuss the two complementary and overlapping systems of oppression, namely, Zionist settler colonialism, with its intent to eliminate the native through ethnic cleansing, displacement, dispossession, and incarceration, and Israeli apartheid, today's legal apparatus that ensures the continued disenfranchisement of the

Palestinians following the onset of al-Nakba. In this context, apartheid must be understood as a tool of Zionism, the latter being the political movement and ideology which emerged in late nineteenth-century Europe and aimed at establishing a Jewish state in the land of Palestine. And an awareness of how settler colonialism and apartheid manifest themselves in gendered ways must pervade every analysis of the circumstances of the Palestinian people and their liberation struggle. Such analysis is central to the discussion of Indigenous issues on Turtle Island, for example, where it is understood that Native women bear the brunt of white supremacist violence. It is also understood when one looks at the Black community, where women and gender non-conforming individuals fall at the intersection of multiple oppressive systems, leading to the observation that "If black women were free, it would mean that everyone else would have to be free since our freedom would necessitate the destruction of all the systems of oppression."[18] I argue, with *Tal'at*, the Palestinian grassroots movement against femicide, that there can be "no free homeland without free women," and that Palestinian women's agency and socio-political location at the intersection of settler colonialism, hypermilitarism, patriarchy, and apartheid, must be the springboard for a discussion of full Palestinian decolonial liberation.[19] I also argue that queers must always be included in any analysis of heteropatriarchy and gendered violence.

To have this complex discussion, we must foreground how the Palestinian struggle is an anticolonial struggle. Doing so challenges the exceptionalism of the Zionist discourse, which would present Israel as a redemptive democracy rising out of the ashes of Europe's antisemitism, rather than a settler colonial nation born of Europe's imperialist ideology. One way I debunk Israel's exceptionalism is by consistently discussing it alongside other countries—primarily the USA and South Africa—to show how Israel is similar to other racist, settler colonial "exceptional" countries. Only after the Palestinian struggle is rightly situated in a global context, alongside other Indigenous struggles for sovereignty and self-determination, can we then move on to a nuanced discussion of apartheid, elaborating on the similarities and differences between the Israeli and South African systems. With a view to foregrounding today's organizing, our analysis will then look back to last century's struggle to overthrow South Africa's apartheid, so as to guide today's activism for freedom, dignity, and sovereignty for the entirety of the Palestinian people: women, men, and gender non-conforming individuals, in the homeland and the diaspora.

Because settler colonialism, state-sanctioned violence, and femicide are co-constitutive evils, the Palestinian struggle must also be understood as a feminist struggle, and an intersectional abolitionist struggle. Thus, this book highlights the agency of Palestinian women in countering colonialism from the days of the British Mandate to the present, and most often doing so by imagining and enacting alternatives to its violence. They are the mothers and daughters who hold extended families together, the freedom fighters, the organizers and sustainers of *intifadas*, the political prisoners, the hundreds of thousands of heroes unknown outside of their intimate circles, as well as the better-known poets, novelists, scholars, and lawyers.

Palestinian women's resistance to foreign imposition is not a new phenomenon. They have participated in anticolonial protests since the early 1920s, when it became clear the British Mandate would facilitate their dispossession. In the late 1930s, when British troops stormed the militant village of Baqa al-Gharbiyya, and rounded up and took away the men, unarmed Palestinian women descended upon the barracks where these men had been detained, securing their release.[20] Decades later, under Israeli occupation, women were instrumental in organizing the grassroots clandestine network and popular committees that sustained the First Intifada, a mass mobilization which forced the world to recognize the Palestinian right to self-determination. Women formed and staffed mobile health clinics, they taught underground classes when Israel shut down schools in collective punishment of the revolting Palestinians, they prepared and delivered food to the youth on the frontlines.[21] Sadly, their forward-looking grassroots leadership was marginalized following the 1993 Oslo Accords, which facilitated the return of the leadership of Palestinian male politicians who clearly lacked the transformative imagination necessary to get us out of the morass of the "peace process." It is impossible not to notice the difference between

the first and second intifadas, especially along gender lines, a difference due in no small part to the creation of the repressive Palestinian
Authority in 1994. Yet, women are still at the forefront of organizing
today, challenging the gendered violence of settler colonialism, as well
as restrictive Palestinian cultural norms. No analysis of Palestinian resistance is complete without focused attention on their interventions.

* * *

It is impossible to overemphasize that today's activism must be *transformational*. It must be decolonial, seeking full liberation from the mental
and generational shackles of the oppressive system, and not merely
anticolonial, aimed at ousting the occupier. Achieving justice for Palestine entails more than abolishing Israeli apartheid. The inertia of over a
century of inequality, and of the privileged status of the settlers as they
forcibly and violently dispossessed, and continue to dispossess, Palestine's Indigenous people, cannot be reversed solely through the formal
dissolution of the oppressive system. The present plight of formerly
colonized countries around the globe, after they gained their independence, as well as the ongoing circumstances of the Black and Indigenous
people of North America, who theoretically have equal rights but who
have remained criminalized, hunted, caged, and murdered, is proof that
eliminating legal barriers without addressing the practical consequences
of injustice does not redress historic inequities. Therefore, even as we
are organizing to overthrow Israel's state-sanctioned violence, we must
look beyond apartheid as the primary means of oppression of the Palestinian people. Beyond apartheid, Zionism itself must be abolished. It is
an essentially racist, supremacist ideology, and the oppressive system it
has produced cannot be reformed.

Abolition hinges on the understanding that reform—making changes
to an existing system—does not solve the problems created by that
system, it only helps maintain the system by making it less obviously
abrasive, without transforming its corrosive core. Today, this argument
is being made about the police all across the USA, with a number of
grassroots organizers and public intellectuals debunking myths that

the police are an overall positive social force, where rogue elements occasionally go awry. Abolitionists argue instead that the system is not broken, it is functioning exactly as it was always intended to. Therefore, there is no need to "fix" it, to restore it to its original form, because that form itself is oppressive at its inception, as it remains to this day. When was "the system" not broken, abolitionists ask? When was it not racist, when was it not violent, when we know that the origin of the police forces in the US South was as slave patrols, while in the US north, they were first established to thwart protests for better labor conditions?

The call for abolishing the police, and prisons, is not recent, having been discussed in the USA for example, almost twenty years ago by Angela Davis in *Are Prisons Obsolete?*, and by anti-carceral grassroots groups such as Critical Resistance, and INCITE! Feminists of Color Against Violence, who understood that their communities are endangered, not protected, by the "security state." However, abolition has now entered popular discourse, with organizers demanding at protests nationally that police forces be defunded, and the abolitionist Mariame Kaba writing an OpEd published in the *New York Times* titled "Yes, We Mean Literally Abolish the Police".[22] Police abolitionists are very clear about the necessity of building strong structures to support disenfranchised communities that have never been "served and protected" by the police. As Angela Davis writes: "Abolition is about organizing community alternatives to policing and mass incarceration, about using the breathing room afforded by these small victories not to propose a slightly better version of the same, but to shoot for something radically different."[23]

In the context of Palestine, abolition hinges on the understanding that a reform of the Zionist state cannot possibly solve the problems created by Zionism, it only helps maintain them. Seeking to reform the Zionist state assumes that Zionism's initial impulse—which is premised on settler colonialism and necessitates land theft, dispossession, displacement, human and cultural genocide—is acceptable, but that something went wrong, somewhere down the line. For instance, a reform limited to the West Bank and Gaza implies that al-Nakba— Palestine's catastrophe—did not start around 1948, but in 1967.

Ending the occupation of the West Bank and Gaza Strip would not dismantle Jewish supremacy in those parts of the Palestinian homeland first occupied in 1948; nor would it address the Right of Return of Palestinians displaced from those cities and villages occupied in 1948, without which the Zionist dream would not have materialized. Indeed, the "peace process," with its endless round of futile talks, is an illustration of the attempt at "reform," rather than abolition. What that process has led to is an entrenchment of dispossession, now subcontracted to the Palestinian Authority. Instead, one must ask: "When was Zionism not a supremacist ideology privileging some people over others, based on perceived ethnicity? When did Zionism not necessitate the ethnic cleansing of the Palestinian people? Was there ever one brief moment, from its inception to the present day, when Zionism was not violent?" Zionism cannot be reformed; it must be abolished.

And abolition in the context of Palestine, as in all contexts, also presumes that one is working to set up the alternative at the very same time one is dismantling the oppressive system. The many initiatives developed by Palestinians today are radically different from what governments have been proposing and supporting since before 1948. Farmers are already establishing sustainable, community supported agriculture. Educators are crafting liberatory and inclusive curricula. Feminists are setting up the infrastructure for a post-Zionist society that is also post-patriarchal. Public intellectuals are crafting detailed proposals that rise above partitions and borders. And Palestinians, both in the diaspora and the homeland, are forming global alliances around causes that bring us together, rather than set us apart. This book discusses some of these while exposing the irreconcilability of Zionism with justice, sustainability, feminism, liberation.

By looking beyond apartheid, and beyond Zionism, we can start envisioning the future of Palestine, one that is beyond various binaries, whether these be the obsolete "two states" delusion, or the "homeland" and the "diaspora" division, or even "Jews" and "Arabs," as if these were mutually exclusive, rather than a colonial invention. Historically, these binaries have been used to divide, yet they have also always had inherently blurred boundaries and criteria. This is evident in the fact that even fourth-generation Palestinian refugees, whether in the Gaza Strip, or in Seattle, Washington, always recall the city or village their families were displaced from. Moreover, a refugee from Yaffa, in present-day Israel, would not be "returning" to their hometown if they were to move to the West Bank, where the new state of Palestine is to be located, according to the ever elusive "two-state solution." Nor would someone from Haifa be "returning" to Khan Younis, in the Gaza Strip, also envisioned as part of that new, amputated Palestine. They would still be displaced, denied the right to return to their homes. Palestine has historically existed as the land between the Jordan River and the Mediterranean Sea, and partial liberation is not justice denied, it is, quite simply, impossible. This is why, following decades of governments and politicians attempting to establish an independent Palestinian "state," Palestine's public intellectuals and activists are looking outside the framework of a two-state solution, to explore nationhood in the context of decolonization, instead of state building. This is the transformative vision that accompanies abolitionist calls, and which we are already witnessing among Palestinian feminist organizers.

From Gaza to Ramallah to Haifa, to New York City and Oakland, California, as a people, we Palestinians are united in our yearning for liberation. Yet, for those of us living in the Global North, we have also joined ranks with other racialized, marginalized, and oppressed communities because our circumstances align us with the surveilled, the criminalized, the disenfranchised, the communities seeking to make this world a better place for all of us, not just a good place for the privileged few.

In today's rapidly evolving context, it is imperative that organizers and activists tend to the many fronts simultaneously, and intentionally, so as to set the foundations for a future Palestine that avoids the trappings of the always-struggling postcolonial nation states of the twentieth century. Black solidarity with Palestine is longstanding, having found its clearest expressions during the Civil Rights movement, when the Student Nonviolent Coordinating Committee (SNCC), the Black Panthers, Angela Y. Davis, Malcolm X, Kwame Ture (formerly Stokely Carmichael), Audre Lorde June Jordan, and Muhammad Ali, among many others, supported the Palestinian people, while African leaders from Nelson Mandela to Kwame Nkrumah also supported Palestinian liberation. More recently, Black–Palestinian solidarity has been injected with renewed energy in the wake of the hypermilitarization of US police, the latter being due in no small part to their joint training with Israeli security forces. And a recent statement by The Red Nation collective opens with the assertion that "Palestine is the moral barometer of Indigenous North America."[24] Meanwhile, Palestinians in the homeland and the global diaspora are actively educating themselves about the struggles of Black and Brown communities around the world and sending tips on confronting police violence from the Gaza Strip to Ferguson, Missouri. In this book, I explore the hopeful arc of this new type of activism, as I discuss how today's intersectional, joint struggles are paving the way to a dignified life for all.

As I challenge the dominant discourse on the question of Palestine, I also intentionally ground my analysis in the writings of grassroots organizers in the USA, as well as the many stellar Palestinian scholars, activists, and organizers who have carved out the space for this discussion. Many of my sources are also Palestinian, rather than from the Global North, even when the latter are available. In an era where we rightly want to hear primarily from queer, and/or Black, and/or Indigenous peoples about their lived experiences, the plight of the Palestinian people remains one of the few instances where observations by outsiders are considered more valid than inside knowledge and scholarship. This is not to dismiss the value of some important contributions by non-Palestinians, but hinges instead on my conviction that we must practice decolonization in scholarship and discourse, as much as in natural resources such as land and water. Just as the Western narrative has long dominated the discourse on Palestine, so have non-Western voices been valued in the West over the voices of Palestinians, who should be the ones articulating their own experiences, analysis, and hopes. This is especially the case in writings critical of Israel, where Jewish allies who denounce Israel's crimes are given more prominent platforms than Palestinians who resist and survive Israel's crimes. The valuing of allied scholarship over Indigenous knowledge is passé, and should be stopped, and reversed, just as colonialism itself must be stopped, and reversed. And the myopic denunciation of the micro level of gendered violence, which would look at "conservative Arab culture" but not at the broader level of gendered violence of settler colonialism, is no longer acceptable. Finally, to marginalize the analysis of women's contributions in an "accessory" chapter, rather than as part and parcel of our collective *sumoud* and the beacon of our full liberation, is no longer admissible.

A Note on Terminology

Throughout this book, I use Palestine to refer to the entirety of the country, from the Jordan River to the Mediterranean Sea. The nation has existed for thousands of years, and continues to exist to this day. The fact that Israel currently occupies that land changes the political status of Palestine, but not its existence. Additionally, the growing recognition that there will never be two states between the river and the sea, that the unity of the Palestinian people cannot be interrupted despite political and geographic fragmentation and that the decolonial worldview that goes beyond the concept of the nation state is a necessary condition of self-determination, all confirm the view that Palestine cannot be divided. I do not put Israel in quotation marks because I am more interested in dismantling Zionism than questioning the legitimacy of the country. Besides, I do not exceptionalize Israel, and would otherwise have to use quotations marks around the names of too many settler colonial countries (the USA, Canada, Australia, all the Latin and South American countries) to be consistent. I also use Turtle Island to refer to North America whenever I am discussing Indigenous matters, that name being based on a common North American Indigenous creation story. And I use the USA when I am referring to the settler colonial country occupying part of that continent. Finally, in the case of the Indigenous people of Turtle Island, I use Indigenous and Native Americans interchangeably, as both terms appear equally in the literature I have read.

1

Settler Colonialism and Indigenous Resistance from Palestine to Turtle Island

In May of 2021, Israeli settlers were aggressively trying to push Palestinians out of their homes in the Sheikh Jarrah neighborhood of Jerusalem, ahead of moving into the houses themselves. In this round of attempted expulsions, twenty-eight Palestinian families were to be made homeless, in the Zionists' quest to "Judaize" the city that historically had been a haven of diversity. The Moroccan quarter, an extension of the Muslim quarter to the north, was razed by Israeli forces three days after the 1967 Six-Day War. And the Russian Compound, one of the oldest districts in central Jerusalem, featuring a large Russian Orthodox church, is now reduced to an Israeli detention and interrogation center, al-Moskobiyeh, notorious for its dungeon cells and harsh methods of torture. The transformation is such that few Palestinians today recall that al-Moskobiyeh, ("the Moscovite," taking its name from "Moscow") was once a residential neighborhood—indeed, the neighborhood my own father was born and grew up in. Thus, when I visited Jerusalem in 2005, and asked to be taken to al-Moskobiyeh, my younger Palestinian guides were puzzled by my request, and joked that nobody should ever "want" to go there.

In Sheikh Jarrah in 2021, in an exchange captured on cell phone and widely circulated on social media, twenty-two-year-old Muna el-Kurd tells Yaacob Fauci, a Long Island, New York-born Israeli settler, that he is stealing her home, to which he responds: "If I don't steal it, someone else will steal it." Fauci explains that he "didn't do this" himself and asks why she is upset with him personally. In this colonizer's mind, Palestinians are fated to be dispossessed, so why shouldn't he be the one stealing the el-Kurd family's home, where he had been squatting for ten years?

I intentionally devote the first chapter of this book to a discussion of settler colonialism, meaning land theft, rather than to apartheid, the legal structure that maintains the supremacy of the land thieves, in order to foreground a characteristic of Zionism that has been eclipsed by the rise of the apartheid framing, namely, that the movement is, from the onset, a European colonial project, which gradually evolved to become a more generally "Western" imperial project, sustained by the USA. I believe it is critically important to discuss the early writings of Zionism, and demonstrate how it was always intended to dispossess the Palestinian people. I do so because many liberals insist that Israel, as a country, is a redemptive project, and that the only problem is "the occupation," meaning Israel's expansion post 1967 into the parts of historical Palestine that were not within the original boundaries of the young state. In the liberal Western mindset, the occupation of lands seized in 1967 is illegal, but Israel within the UN-determined 1947 borders is legitimate, because imperial powers deemed it so. But the Israeli theft of Palestinian land did not start in 1967. Seventy percent of the Palestinian people lost their homes and became refugees in 1948, not 1967. The ethnic cleansing we are witnessing today is merely a continuation of what began under the British Mandate, and culminated in the large-scale displacement of Palestinians in 1947–1948. The Zionist "system" is not broken, it was always a racist, supremacist, settler colonial project.

Yaacob Fauci had been recruited by Nahalat Shimon International, a US-based settler organization that seeks to ethnically cleanse Jerusalem of its non-Jewish population. Like other settler organizations, Nahalat Shimon International first sends out a group of young adult men to live in Palestinian houses, harassing the Palestinian owners until the families leave, at which point Jewish Israeli families take over. Other settler organizations include The Israel Land Fund, which facilitates Jewish acquisition of Palestinian homes that it claims on its website "are currently being squatted on by Arabs who have built on them ilegally [sic] or are renting."[1] Another settler organization, Regavim, specializes in pressuring the Israeli government into demolishing Bedouin struc-

17

tures in the Naqab, as well as Palestinian homes in the West Bank. Yet another settler organization seeking to take over Palestinian homes is Ateret Cohanim, whose Director of Community Development and Outreach, David Mark, has said that "at the end of the day, it is not the Jewish people who are the occupiers or thieves, but rather the European created 'Palestinian' people who are the real occupiers."[2] These settler organizations—and there are others—all empower Zionist Jews to take over Palestinian homes, presenting the dispossession of Palestinians as "ideological reclamation" of Jewish land.

The el-Kurds' problem is representative of the plight of numerous Palestinians caught in the Israeli legal system, which routinely denies them permits to build, then appropriates their houses, or orders them demolished, even as it facilitates the construction of Jewish-only settlements, which are illegal under international law. Specifically, the el-Kurds are among some of the Palestinian families displaced in 1948 who were given modest homes in Sheikh Jarrah in 1956 per an agreement between the United Nations Relief and Works Agency for Palestinian Refugees (UNRWA) and the Jordanian government. As the families grew, some, including the el-Kurds, built extensions to their homes. Numbering eight family members in 1999, the el-Kurds had applied to Israel for a permit to build an extra room, but the Jerusalem municipality would not even consider the request. The el-Kurds went ahead and built the extension anyway. In 2009, Israel ruled against them, fined them close to $100,000, forbade them to use the room, and instead allowed the settlers to move into that extension, separated from the family by a mere drywall. The dispute in 2021 was about the settlers taking over the entire house. Fauci himself had been squatting there for ten years, hence the "first-name basis" conversation between him and Muna el-Kurd. This intimacy, by the way, should put an end to the delusion that the "conflict would be resolved if only Jews and Palestinians got to know each other." Besides, settler colonialism, land theft, displacement, and occupation of a family's home should never be referred to as a "conflict."

But the el-Kurds were determined not to move out, no matter how difficult life with the settlers was. Muna el-Kurd's grandmother, Rifqa, who died in June 2020 at the ripe age of 103, was representative of Palestinian *sumoud* and the insistence on the right of return. As Muna el-Kurd's twin brother Muhammed writes, Rifqa was "older than Israel itself. For this, she was hailed as the 'icon of Palestinian resistance' by Jerusalemites. During the 1948 Nakba, she left her home meticulously cleaned, not knowing she would be readying it for its colonizers."[3] El-Kurd, author of a poetry book named after his grandmother, recalls her, at "80-something," as a "freedom fighter, an ambulance and a half, treating tear-gassed protestors with yogurt and onions."[4] Rifqa el-Kurd had famously said she would only leave her Sheikh Jarrah home to return to the one she had fled in 1948, in Haifa.

But in 2021, in Haifa, Ramle, and Lydd, cities seized by Zionist fighters in 1948, Israelis were once again roaming the streets, looking for homes with Arab names, threatening to attack them at night. Lynch mobs chanting "Death to Arabs" enjoyed the protection of the Israeli gendarmes and "Border Control" officers—an ironic misnomer as Israel does not have recognized borders—who later rounded up the Palestinian protestors, rather than the Jewish mobs. And the Gaza Strip, which had been sealed off from the rest of the world for close to fourteen years, came yet again under Israeli military assault, with air strikes and a threatened ground invasion. Palestinians took to the streets in the West Bank, protesting Israel's actions within the 1948 borders, as well as against the Gaza Strip, in a show of national unity against colonialism not seen since the revolt of 1936–1939. The terror experienced by Palestinians throughout the homeland equaled that of the catastrophic years from 1947–1948. Yet, there was also a new feeling of defiance, of guarded optimism, a nascent belief that liberation was within reach. The hopefulness was due in no small part to the youthful grassroots leadership, acting in defiance of both Israeli police forces and the Palestinian Authority, which was determined to quash the protests.[5] And both in the homeland, and in various parts of the global diaspora, the leadership of the "Unity Uprising" was overwhelmingly women, and queers.

Also in 2021, while most cities in the USA held rallies and protests on May 15, the customary al-Nakba commemoration day, Seattle's rally was held on May 16. This is because the organizers, the feminist collective called Falastiniyyat, had learned that an Indigenous group was holding a rally for Missing and Murdered Indigenous Women on May 15, and they did not want to compete with it, distract from it, or otherwise dilute its importance.[6] For their May 16 rally, Falastiniyyat also made sure they featured Indigenous speakers, as well as Black, Filipinx, and, of course, Palestinian speakers. I was the first speaker following the Indigenous land acknowledgement, and the poet Lena Khalaf Tuffaha was the last one, so that Palestinian women framed the speeches to the crowd. "We don't want to make it all about Palestine," one of the rally organizers told me, adding: "We are very intentional about highlighting the global joint struggles against imperialism, state-sanctioned racism, and colonialism." Throughout Turtle Island, Palestinian groups had been centering Indigenous voices, out of an understanding of joint struggle, along with a sense of obligation to the rightful stewards of the land. Falastiniyyat itself had formed in 2020 in response to toxic masculinity in the local Palestinian organizing scene. Their commitment to the indivisibility of justice, and refusal to co-opt other communities' struggles, is typical of today's Palestinian feminist organizing. The Old Guard is being made redundant, obsolete, not by direct attack, but rather through the creation of an alternative that attracts those who have been disheartened by the "peace process," by patriarchy, by a focus on Palestine that fails to encompass and support other struggles. This is abolitionist practice in action, creating the alternative at the very same time as it dismantles oppressive systems.

At the Seattle rally, as elsewhere across the USA, the flags and signs carried by protestors, and counter-protestors, revealed common affinities and synergies, showing who was in coalition with whom. The Palestine rights rallies invariably included Black Lives Matter, Indigenous Sovereignty, Refugee Rights, anti-imperialist Filipinx organizers and activists, and in larger cities like Chicago and New York, there were flags from Ireland, Puerto Rico, Columbia, Argentina, Haiti, and many more countries. Banners with variations of the slogan "End the US War Machine, from Palestine to the Philippines" punctuated the red, black, white, and green of the Palestinian flag. Meanwhile, the pro-Israel rallies were a sea of blue and white, Israel's flag with the Star of David in the center, with some American stars and stripes flags, and, predictably by now, a few Trump flags, and some confederate flags. The Indigenous, the colonized, the disenfranchised and criminalized, side with the Palestinians; the white supremacist colonizers side with Israel, as they are attracted to the exclusive ethnic character and violent practices of the state. Indeed, according to his social media profile, Fauci, the settler who was squatting in the el-Kurd family home, is a fan of former President Donald Trump. In 2017, white supremacist Richard Spencer, the de facto leader of the alt-right in the USA, had explained to an Israeli news anchor that:

> an Israeli citizen, someone who understands your identity, who has a sense of nationhood and peoplehood, and the history and experience of the Jewish people, you should respect someone like me, who has analogous feelings about whites. You could say that I am a white Zionist—in the sense that I care about my people, I want us to have a secure homeland for us and ourselves. Just like you want a secure homeland in Israel.[7]

The less sophisticated Zionists, such as Yaacob Fauci, openly associate with the US alt-right. However, when it comes to "debating" the "complicated" question of Palestine and the legitimacy of Israel, more sophisticated Zionists seek to distance themselves from white supremacists, and have gradually adopted the discourse of indigeneity. Thus, they would claim that all Jews globally are descended from historic Palestine, hence making "aliyah" (the Zionist term for Jewish immigration to Israel) always a "return" to their ancestral land. Many are offended at the suggestion that people not of Eastern Mediterranean stock could at any point have converted to Judaism, even when there is a historical record of such group conversions, from San Nicandro, Italy, to the Khazars of central Asia, as well as individual conversions, generally women marrying a Jewish spouse.[8] Additionally, these sophisticated Zionists insist that they *alone* are the Indigenous peoples of that land, with the Palestinians being the interlopers. More recently, Afrikaners have been converting to Judaism so as to become settlers in Palestine, where their new religious identification offers them the privileges they previously had as whites in apartheid South Africa. It would be interesting to hear the sophisticated Zionists' explanation of this phenomenon—their mental gymnastics are often fascinating. I once debated with a "New Age Zionist" who told me there is a lot of science we still can't understand, and that deeply held religious beliefs change a person's DNA, hence, they concluded that converting to Judaism makes you Semitic. I had to point out that "semitism" is not a genetic trait; it is a linguistic group.

However, the Zionist claim to indigeneity has not been a constant of that ideology. Rather, it reflects a recent opportunistic trend to align with one of the core causes of today's progressive grassroots. In the nineteenth century, the early Zionist ideologues viewed themselves as being "spiritually connected" to the land where Judaism originated, rather than as "Indigenous" to Palestine. They were children of their age, jumping aboard the European colonial train as they sought to create a nation of their own. Their discourse, as they envisioned, and pursued sponsorship of their project, was that of their moment: they intended to colonize Palestine. They may have been latecomers to colonialism but, in the late nineteenth century, they were not yet fully anachronistic.

In very broad strokes, colonialism can be divided into two types. One is economic colonialism, or "franchise colonialism," to use Patrick Wolfe's terms, where the colonial power exploits the natural resources of its colony, without trying to transform that country beyond what is necessary for colonial profit.[9] The colonizers in this case always identify with the metropole, they do not take on a new identity, nor do they seek to establish roots in the country they are exploiting, even if they live their entire lives there. A prime example of economic colonialism is Britain's imperial rule over India, which lasted centuries, but where the local cultures were only modified with a view to better serve Britain's imperial interests. Any changes introduced into India, from the railroad tracks to schooling and the communication infrastructure now benefiting the elite Indian social classes, were meant to optimize British trade interests in the metropole. And the English families in India never claimed to have become Indian, or anything other than English. Settler colonialism, on the other hand, "destroys to replace."[10] Examples of settler colonialism abound globally, from the Americas to Australia and New Zealand. These countries today have non-native languages, religions, and worldviews as the primary denominators, having sought to replace the Indigenous peoples and their cultures. The descendants of the colonizers there have taken on a new identity, and now identify as American, Brazilian, Australian, South African. Their allegiance is no longer to the metropole, but to the new country they are building atop the Indigenous people's cultural artifacts. Even before these distinctions between different types of colonialism had been articulated in scholarly discourse, it was clear that the vision for Israel would be one of a settler colonial nation, an endeavor that requires the destruction of the pre-existing people, and their culture, in order to create a new country. The Palestinian people would be "spirited away," as Theodor Herzl wrote in 1895, and Palestine would become Israel.[11] The prime example Zionist ideologues had in mind was not India, it was the United States of America.

The USA's very existence hinges on a foundational contradiction. It was viewed by the settlers as a land of refuge, yet it engaged in multiple genocidal attacks on the Indigenous peoples, and repeatedly displaced those who had survived the merciless massacres and brutal warfare. The USA's ongoing "elimination" of the Indigenous people is obvious today in their disproportionate representation in the prison system, where they have the highest incarceration rates of any ethnic and racial group. Indigenous Americans also serve the most life sentences, an indication of the US "justice" system's desire to put them away for as long as possible. A 2015 report shows that Indigenous youth, who make up 1 percent of the total American youth population, account to 70 percent of youth committed to the Federal Bureau of Prisons. Additionally, Native Americans are more likely to be killed by police than members of any other group.[12] The cultural genocide of Indigenous nations is most obvious today in the ongoing removal of children from their families and their placement in the foster care system, where they are also disproportionately represented, and where they frequently get adopted by white families. This is clearly a continuation of the colonizers' desire to eradicate Indigenous culture, earlier enacted through the residential schools that tried to "kill the Indian, save the man."

The USA has also historically been extremely selective as to who would be granted refuge. Jews, for example, were not welcome in the New England colonies, except for Newport, Rhode Island. In the twentieth century, Jews escaping Hitler's Germany were still being turned away by the USA. The Chinese Exclusion Act of 1882 long pre-dates the Muslim ban of the twenty-first century. The new country was expansionist, as it continued to dispossess and disenfranchise the Indigenous people, in the European settlers' aggressive quest for more territory. Yet, it claimed to be itself coming under attack by the Indigenous nations defending their ancestral lands. This reversal of reality is inscribed in the US Declaration of Independence, which states that the King of England "has endeavoured to bring on the inhabitants of our frontiers, the merciless Indian Savages, whose known rule of warfare, is an undistinguished destruction of all ages, sexes and conditions." And, of course, the newly born nation claimed to be a democracy, asserting its belief that "all men are created equal," while deeming the Indigenous peoples "savages," enslaving Africans and their children, and depriving all women of the most basic human rights.

Israel would follow the American model. Its proponents had always envisioned it as a new nation, replacing the pre-existing one: settler colonialism, which necessitates the elimination of the native. Zionism was not "franchise colonialism," no Zionist ideologue articulated a vision of Jews extracting resources from Palestine to enrich Germany, Austria, Poland, or Russia. The Jewish colonizers, wherever they lived in Europe (Arab Jews were rarely considered in the early discussions and, in those instances, typically were regarded in racist colonial terms) would emigrate to Palestine, and make it Israel, a Jewish nation. A selective "land of refuge," which destroyed to replace. The Palestinians, like the various Indigenous peoples of the Americas, were to disappear. Their resistance, in defense of their own ancestral lands, would render them "terrorists," as it had rendered Turtle Island's Indigenous nations into "savages" attacking settlers on the settlers' self-claimed frontiers. And just as the European settlers in Turtle Island did not spare the Indigenous based on age or sex, yet claimed it was those "merciless savages" whose practice "is an undistinguished destruction of all ages, sexes and conditions," so Israel spared no Palestinian on the basis of age or sex.

In her meticulously documented book, *Our American Israel*, Amy Kaplan illustrates how Israel's founding narrative projected the first Zionists as "pioneers" with a "frontier mentality," pushing the aboriginal peoples out of the way of the progress they were bringing to a benighted land.[13] This shared ethos would ultimately secure American support for Israel. As British diplomat Richard Crossman put it, when he first realized how much support Israel had among Americans: "Because our own history conditions our political thinking, Americans, all other things being equal, will always give their sympathy to the pioneer."[14] That initial American sympathy with Israel—based on political thinking conditioned by a similar history—was reinforced by the Zionist narrative, as circulated in popular culture. Kaplan, like many other scholars of the Zionist metanarrative in the USA, examines the impact of Leon Uris' 1958 bestselling novel, made into the 1960 star-studded blockbuster film, *Exodus*, which presented Israel to mainstream Americans in terms they understood and identified with. The film, like the novel, "reenacted the primal myth of the American frontier," asserting that the violence of the hero, the Israeli cowboy, is itself a response to that of the Other.[15] "It is the barbarism of the Other—whether Indian or Arab—that forces the hero to become violent; he adopts their methods in order to defeat them, and to establish a border between legitimate and illegitimate violence," Kaplan explains.[16] The star of that movie was America's heart-throb, Paul Newman. That he was a white, blue-eyed Midwesterner, with a last name that was as gentile as it was potentially Jewish, only added to the immense appeal of the movie, as it presented the main Jewish character as an irresistibly handsome young male, at a time when much of the West was experiencing extreme guilt at having allowed the Holocaust to happen.[17] The violence that Newman's character, Ari Ben Canaan, engaged in was "legitimate violence," to use Max Weber's concept of the state, or in this case, the proto-state, having a monopoly of violence; consequently, all resistance to it was "illegitimate."[18] The seeds of the West describing Palestinian resistance as offensive, rather than defensive, had been planted through the parallels with the USA, which had viewed Indigenous resistance to dispossession as "attacks" by the "merciless savages." Today, we see this reversal of accountability in mainstream Western media reports that mention Israel "responding to Palestinian attacks," with no mention of the fact that Israel has been violating Palestinian human rights, and occupying Palestinian land, for decades, not the other way around.

Despite its many historical inaccuracies, and its total glossing over Palestinian dispossession, *Exodus*, as Edward Said commented in 2001, still provides "the main narrative model that dominates American thinking" about the foundation of the State of Israel.[19] Twenty years after Said decried the unfortunate impact of *Exodus* on mainstream American thinking, the book is still, for many Americans, their only narrative about the birth of Israel and, as such, continues to fulfill the Zionist propaganda role its author intended. Another of its insidious effects, which has not received enough attention, is its offensive homogenizing of Arabs as fumbling incompetent fools, setting the tone for the negative stereotyping of Arabs pervasive in most Hollywood films to this day. Jack Shaheen's *Reel Bad Arabs: How Hollywood Vilifies a People* is a must watch documentary on the topic.[20]

Meanwhile, Ari Ben Canaan represents the ideal of "the New Jew." The newly founded Israel was turning the long-standing European stereotype of the "diminutive," "effeminate," "shady" Jew into a strong, muscular, masculine man. Oz Almog's book, *The Sabra: The Creation of the New Jew* is revealing of the misogyny pervasive in Zionist ideology, as it looks exclusively at traditionally masculine figures such as the Palmach commander, the marine commando, the pilot—all male roles at the time—in its discussion of "the first Israelis."[21] Women, apparently, did not qualify. Indeed, Almog's entire book on "the New Jew" does not have any discussion of early Israeli women's contributions, with chapters titled "The Elect Son [but not daughter] of the Chosen People," "The Stamp of His [not hers] Country's Landscape," "Uri [not Ruth] of Arabia," and "Monks [but not nuns] in Khaki." Today, the settlers taking over Palestinian homes are also generally young men, members of any of several settler organizations, who occupy a Palestinian home until the neighborhood is deemed ready to be occupied by Israeli families. They are the "pioneers" of the twenty-first century, single men, or married with a wife and children awaiting word that they can now move into the house a Palestinian family was evicted from.

Colonialism is always gendered, and always sexually violent. The very language used by colonizers reflects the sexualization of conquest. Throughout Africa, they described their forays as "penetration" into "virgin" land—"virgin" because new to Europeans. But the violence was not a metaphor. The colonizers' attacks were invariably accompanied by "rape, loot, and pillage." Women who survived the rapes were frequently taken hostage, as sex slaves. From Okinawa to Korea to the Philippines, Iraq, and Afghanistan, entire micro economies of human trafficking and sex work are set up around military bases, to "serve" the troops. "Man camps," the temporary housing for men working in oil, mining, forestry, and other extractive industries primarily around Indigenous reservations today, are hot beds of rape, with nearby Indigenous women frequently targeted because of the rapists' sadly valid assumption that they will not be arrested and persecuted. In Palestine, women were not spared the masculinist violence of Zionism. Today, there is ample documentation that, from the onset of al-Nakba to the present day, their experiences reveal the multiple jeopardy of being colonized, and being women. From the rapes that accompanied the attacks on towns and villages from 1947 to 1949, to the sexual torture of political prisoners in Israeli jails, to the rape, mutilation, and evisceration of refugee women in Sabra and Shatila, and the denial of reproductive justice throughout the West Bank, Palestinian women have borne the brunt of Israel's sexual violence. And queer Palestinians have not been spared in the supposedly "gay friendly" Jewish state, where homonationalism means openly gay Israelis can serve in the occupation army, but where, as Palestinian queers have repeatedly noted, there is "no pink door in the apartheid wall."[22] Homonationalism, or the assimilation of "acceptable gays," will be further discussed below.

Before we elaborate on the gendered violence of settler colonialism, it is helpful to return to the shift in the Zionist narrative, from colonizer to Indigenous, and from cowboy to "Indian," a shift that reveals, yet again, the theft and appropriation Israel hinges on.

A Colonial Enterprise

Early Zionism was fully reconciled to the fact that it was a colonial movement, modeled upon the European colonization of various countries, including North America. Early Zionist thinker Ze'ev Jabotinsky, for example, equates Zionism with colonialism when he writes:

My readers have a general idea of the history of colonisation in other countries. I suggest that they consider all the precedents with which they are acquainted, and see whether there is one solitary instance of any colonisation being carried on with the consent of the native population. There is no such precedent.

The native populations, civilised or uncivilised, have always stubbornly resisted the colonists, irrespective of whether they were civilised or savage.

It does not matter at all which phraseology we employ in explaining our colonising aims, Herzl's or Sir Herbert Samuel's.

Colonisation carries its own explanation, the only possible explanation, unalterable and as clear as daylight to every ordinary Jew and every ordinary Arab.

Colonisation can have only one aim, and Palestine Arabs cannot accept this aim. It lies in the very nature of things, and in this particular regard nature cannot be changed.

Zionist colonisation must either stop, or else proceed regardless of the native population. Which means that it can proceed and develop only under the protection of a power that is independent of the native population—behind an iron wall, which the native population cannot breach. ... Zionist colonisation, even the most restricted, must either be terminated or carried out in defiance of the will of the native population.[23] [italics on official Jabotinsky Institute website]

Jabotinsky, who had served in Palestine as a member of the British Army in 1918, knew there were Palestinians for whom the "colonisation of their country" was inadmissible. But that did not trouble him much, as his vision was in keeping with the imperialism of his day, which openly dismissed the will of the native population. After all, in 1923, as he was writing his essay on Jewish European colonialism of an Arab country, most of the world was colonized by European powers: over 90 percent of Africa, all of Australia, almost all of Polynesia, over 60 percent of Asia, and all of the Americas. Official figures put the percentage of the Americas "under European colonialism" in 1900 at under 30 percent, rather than close to 100 percent. This low figure reflects the fact that countries that had declared their independence from Spain, Portugal, and England in the eighteenth and nineteenth centuries, countries such as Mexico, Brazil, and the USA, were no longer considered "under European colonialism," even though it was the colonizers, not the countries' Indigenous peoples, who were now "independent." It is a similar linguistic slippage that describes the founding of Israel in 1948 as "independence," when that was achieved at the expense of the native population. Jabotinsky's "The Iron Wall" deserves a full, close reading, as it is replete with sober assessments of the Palestinian people's love of their land, and the complete indifference of the European settlers for this love. For example, he writes that the Palestinians "feel at least the same instinctive jealous love of Palestine, as the old Aztecs felt for ancient Mexico, and their [sic] Sioux for their rolling Prairies."[24]

Zionism, thus, clearly originated as a European colonial project, albeit by individuals who identified primarily in terms of their religion, rather than their nationality. This is not a unique development: religious identification has long been a defining factor in European nationalism, from the many "wars of religion" that characterized the sixteenth, seventeenth, and eighteenth century, to the more recent division around support for, or opposition to, the European Union (EU), with Catholics overwhelmingly in support, and Protestants primarily opposed to the EU.[25] Jabotinsky, born in Ukraine, fought with the British Army, where he founded the Jewish Battalion. The native populations, anywhere and everywhere, will resist conquest, he wrote, and do not distinguish between good and bad colonists, as they grasp that the impact of either type will be the same. Yet, in full awareness of the resistance Jewish colonizers would encounter, and the Palestinian people's deep love of their land, he prefaced his 1923 essay, "The Iron Wall," with the assertion: "Colonisation of Palestine: Agreement with Arabs Impossible at Present, Zionism Must Go Forward," and ends it with a sober assessment that such an agreement would only be reached when the Palestinians have been defeated into submission. He writes:

> We cannot offer any adequate compensation to the Palestinian Arabs in return for Palestine. And therefore, there is no likelihood of any voluntary agreement being reached. So that all those who regard such an agreement as a condition sine qua non for Zionism may as well say "non" and withdraw from Zionism.
>
> *Zionist colonisation must either stop, or else proceed regardless of the native population.* Which means that it can proceed and develop only under the protection of a power that is independent of the native population—behind an iron wall, which the native population cannot breach.[26]

Jabotinsky was the founder of "revisionist Zionism" which, unlike the "practical Zionism" of David Ben-Gurion and Chaim Weizmann, respectively Israel's first prime minister and first president, aspired from the very beginning to an expanded Jewish state in Transjordan, meaning all of historic Palestine, as well as land on the East Bank of the Jordan River. In other words, he was aspiring for an Israel even larger than historic Palestine. In a perfect illustration of the essential flaw at the very core of the attempt to reconcile Zionism with democracy, Jabotinsky wanted a Jewish majority in a land inhabited by "a living people," who had to be subdued by an overpowering "iron wall," and whose rights as equal citizens would be respected only after they are subdued (we will return to a discussion of this "iron wall" in Chapter 2). Almost one full century after his influential essay, the reality of present-day Palestine continues to bear witness to the impossibility of reconciling Zionism with respect for the rights of the Indigenous people.

In a lesser known essay, published only one week after "The Iron Wall," and titled "The Ethics of the Iron Wall," Jabotinsky unambiguously calls the Zionist colonial venture "immoral."[27] As an aside, and since some anti-Zionists often eagerly argue that early Zionists had not always looked at Palestine as the country where to establish the "Jewish nation state," it is in "The Ethics of the Iron Wall" that Jabotinsky mentions Uganda as an alternative to Palestine. But his discussion clearly indicates that he was not seriously considering Uganda, as much as just giving an example of any other country, to show that "colonisation in Uganda is also immoral, and colonisation in any other place in the world, whatever it may be called, is immoral."[28] And since it is immoral everywhere, because "There are no more uninhabited islands in the world. In every oasis there is a native population settled from times immemorial, who will not tolerate an immigrant majority or an invasion of outsiders," then why not Palestine, where Judaism originated, and from which Jews had once been expelled?[29] "The Ethics of the Iron Wall" is an interesting sequel to the better known and generally more widely referenced "The Iron Wall," because in the later essay, Jabotinsky states that some Jews were indeed expelled from Palestine, and as such, some would be returning to their ancestral land. However, he also acknowledges that not all the inhabitants of that land were expelled by the ancient Roman Empire, and that today's Palestinians are indeed Indigenous, "from times immemorial." Instead, he describes the Zionist settlers themselves as "an invasion of outsiders."

As he was writing in 1923, after serving in the British Army, and being appointed a member of the Order of the British Empire, Jabotinsky was expressing the views of the dominant European discourse: imperial, colonial, expansionist. He had little patience for "morality," if such morality clashed with his political aspirations. He was writing for fellow Europeans, the vast majority of whom had even less concern for the Indigenous Palestinians than he did. He claims "indifference" to the plight of the Palestinians, not hatred toward them. He could theorize about the best way to subdue a native population, without sounding to his peers like a tyrant. And he was quite aware that "we cannot offer any adequate compensation to the Palestinian Arabs in return for Palestine."[30] That did not trouble him much. Another important chronological observation, which counters the current historical revisionism, is the acknowledgment that these early Zionist plans and aspirations, while fueled by a desire to avoid Europe's antisemitism and the many pogroms in Russia, pre-date the Holocaust. Lord Balfour's 1917 declaration of British royal support for a Jewish state in parts of Palestine did not come in the wake of Hitler's crimes. Jabotinsky's foundational Zionist writings were penned in the 1920s. The Holocaust catalyzed the founding of Israel, but the colonial ambitions expressed by early Zionists are grounded in Europe's eighteenth- and nineteenth-century imperialism, as much as they are a response to Europe's centuries-old antisemitism. Ultimately, as Palestinian historian Sherene Seikaly has noted, Europe's Jews, ostracized for centuries in their own countries, were only allowed access into "the category of the European" upon leaving Europe.[31]

However, within a couple of decades of the founding of Israel, even Western discourse about colonialism had shifted significantly. Ruling with an iron fist over a dispossessed native population was no longer openly acceptable to most European liberals, the stalwarts of Zionism at that time, as they continue to be now. Over thirty African and Asian countries had gained their independence from European powers from 1945 to 1960, others were still fighting for liberation, and the global sentiment favored Indigenous national sovereignty over imperial rule. This is the historical and cultural context that saw a complete shift in Zionist discourse, from one that acknowledged long-standing Indigenous Palestinian life in Palestine, "from times immemorial," to use Jabotinsky's words, to a denial that the Palestinian people even existed. It is at this juncture that "a land without a people for a people without a land" became the most common depiction of Palestine—even as close to 80 percent of the Palestinian people had been displaced, being made landless. As has been amply documented by now, from 1947 to 1948, over 700,000 Palestinians were expelled from their homes, and some five hundred Palestinian towns and villages were razed to the ground.[32] In 1948, that large number accounted for more than three-quarters of the population of Palestine. And to this day, displaced Palestinians make up approximately 70 percent of the Palestinian people. Claiming that the newly colonized country had been "a land without a people" was more convenient, however, once colonialism was no longer viewed as the civilizing mission colonizers had once claimed it to be.

The denial of the long-standing Palestinian presence in our homeland is best illustrated by former Israeli Prime Minister Golda Meir who, in 1969, infamously claimed that the Palestinians simply "did not exist." Meir was responding to a question by a British reporter, who was curious to know how she, as a self-proclaimed caring political leader, felt about the Palestinians who were dispossessed during the creation of Israel. Her answer:

> There were no such thing as Palestinians. When was there an independent Palestinian people with a Palestinian state? It was either southern Syria before the First World War, and then it was a Palestine including Jordan. It was not as though there was a Palestinian people in Palestine considering itself as a Palestinian people and we came and threw them out and took their country from them. They did not exist.[33]

In 1972, a *New York Times* reporter quoted that statement to Meir, asking if she had since changed her mind. Her response: "I said there never was a Palestinian nation. The people who formerly lived in Palestine then lived for 19 years as Jordanian citizens. There were Palestinians in Gaza after 1948 but the Egyptians wouldn't give them Egyptian citizenship."[34]

The Eurocentrism that pervades the Israeli politician's answer, again, recalls that of the early European settlers and colonists who came to the Americas, and claimed that it was theirs for the taking, because they did not recognize the familiar trappings of a European nation state in the Indigenous people's attachment to their ancestral lands. If it takes "an independent nation state," rather than a very deeply rooted attachment to the land, for a people to "exist," then the Indigenous Americans also did not exist. And since they did not exist, as a European-style nation state, then in their resistance they became "merciless savages," attacking

33

the settlers on the settlers' frontiers. Interestingly, Golda Meir, Israel's only female prime minister to date, was voted "most admired woman in America" in a 1974 Gallup poll, placing her before then First Lady Betty Ford, with Pat Nixon, wife of former President Richard Nixon, in third place. The *New York Times* reporter who interviewed Golda Meir in 1972 describes her as "the most formidable woman I have ever met."[35] Frequently described as the Iron Lady of Israel and referred to by David Ben-Gurion as "the best man in the government," Meir consistently distanced herself from the Jewish Israeli women's movement. Having climbed up the political ladder of an aggressive masculinist military state, she could not be bogged down by such trivial matters as equality for women—not even Jewish women. Yet, even though her political agenda never concerned itself with women's issues, she remains a feminist icon for many white feminists, a sad illustration of the fact that Western feminism is about personal advancement, not collective empowerment. Meanwhile, the *Shalvi/Hyman Encyclopedia of Jewish Women* notes, soberly:

> She was, in current parlance, a "queen bee," a woman who climbs to the top, then pulls the ladder up behind her. She did not wield the prerogatives of power to address women's special needs, to promote other women, or to advance women's status in the public sphere. The fact is that at the end of her tenure her Israeli sisters were no better off than they had been before she took office.[36]

But hegemonic white feminism is imperialist at its core, hence the admiration this white colonizer continues to garner among women in Europe and the USA.

The deliberate erasure of Indigenous peoples occurs on multiple levels. In the USA, from New York to New Orleans to Newcastle, many towns and cities today have European names, often preceded with "New," both to mark their difference from their "Old World" affiliation, and to denote the "start-up" nature of the settlement. Thousands of others have Christian names, such as San Diego, Santa Clara, St. Paul, Antioch, and Corpus Christi, establishing the supremacy of the settlers' religion over those of the Indigenous nations. And from Texas to North Dakota, there are a total of twenty-three towns and cities named "Columbus," and a dozen named Virginia, after Queen Elizabeth I, "the virgin queen." A similar renaming of pre-existing Palestinian cities and villages took place with the Israeli conquest, as acknowledged in 1969 by then Defense Minister Moshe Dayan, who remarked:

We came to this country which was already populated by Arabs, and we are establishing a Hebrew, that is a Jewish state here. [...] Jewish villages were built in the place of Arab villages. You do not even know the names of these Arab villages, and I do not blame you, because these geography books no longer exist; the Arab villages are not there either. Nahalal arose in the place of Mahalul, Gevat—in the place of Jibta, Sarid—in the place of Haneifa and Kefar Yehoshua—in the place of Tell Shamam. There is no one place built in this country that did not have a former Arab population.[37]

As Edward Said points out, even while acknowledging the dispossession that is foundational to the establishment of "the Jewish state," Dayan was skipping over the violence that caused the dispossession, the multiple massacres that led to the Palestinians fleeing their villages. A similar erasure happens in American discourse, which acknowledges that the USA was and remains inhabited by Indigenous nations yet fails to mention any massacres in its annual re-enactment of the "thanksgiving" dinner. The historical parallels—albeit centuries apart— between the USA and Israel continue, as some Israelis today justify the dispossession of the Palestinian people, comparing it to the dispossession of the Indigenous nations of Turtle Island, and saying it was for "the greater good." "I feel sympathy for the Palestinian people, which truly underwent a hard tragedy," Israeli historian Benny Morris said in 2004, for example.[38]

I feel sympathy for the refugees themselves. But if the desire to establish a Jewish state here is legitimate, there was no other choice. ... Even the great American democracy could not have been created without the annihilation of the Indians. There are cases in which the overall, final good justifies harsh and cruel acts that are committed in the course of history.[39]

Morris, who has authored several books about Israel's founding, and conducted extensive research into the Israeli Army archives, does not deny the expulsion of the Palestinian people. In an interview with *Haaretz*, Israel's most influential newspaper, he states:

A Jewish state would not have come into being without the uprooting of 700,000 Palestinians. Therefore it was necessary to uproot them. There was no choice but to expel that population. It was necessary to cleanse the hinterland and cleanse the border areas and cleanse the main roads. It was necessary to cleanse the villages from which our convoys and our settlements were fired on.[40]

Indeed, Morris believes that the expulsion of over 700,000 Palestinians was insufficient, and that David Ben-Gurion, who was the military commander of the Zionist fighters in 1948, should have expelled every single Palestinian:

If he was already engaged in expulsion, maybe he should have done a complete job. I know that this stuns the Arabs and the liberals and the politically correct types. But my feeling is that this place would be quieter and know less suffering if the matter had been resolved once and for all. If Ben-Gurion had carried out a large expulsion and cleansed the whole country—the whole Land of Israel, as far as the Jordan River. It may yet turn out that this was his fatal mistake. If he had carried out a full expulsion—rather than a partial one—he would have stabilized the State of Israel for generations.[41]

Does Morris somehow foster the illusion that if an entire people is displaced, rather than the majority of that people, they will forget their homes, towns, villages, and lives before their dispossession? Would the Palestinian people have experienced "less suffering" if every last Palestinian had been expelled? And had Ben-Gurion "cleansed" all of Palestine, would there be stability for Israel today? Notice that justice is not a concern for Morris, nor Palestinian rights, only stability for Israel. At any cost. Including complete ethnic cleansing As such, he is representative of the many Zionists who consider themselves leftist but cannot extend their left-wing ideas to Arabs. Indeed, he gives Albert Camus as an example, saying: "I also identify with Albert Camus. He was considered a left-winger and a person of high morals, but when he referred to the Algerian problem he placed his mother ahead of morality."[42] Camus's *The Stranger*, considered a masterpiece of existentialism, is deeply anti-Arab. And even a superficial reading of Morris's interview immediately negates his illusions of being a leftist.

More recently, Indigenous rights, sovereignty, and self-determination have become important rallying points for progressives, as evidenced, for example, in the groundswell of support for the Standing Rock Sioux tribe in their defiant stance against the desecration of their ancestral grounds. The popular embrace of "Indigenous Peoples' Day," which replaces "Columbus Day," is another expression of the grassroots shift toward an appreciation of native rights. Meanwhile, Israel has lost its progressive veneer, as more and more people support the plight of the Palestinians as a displaced, dispossessed, and disenfranchised Indigenous people. Hence, the Zionist attempt to regain liberal support, through the tactic of "redwashing," or claiming indigeneity for Jewish Israelis, presenting them as the Arab world's "Indians."

For example, in a talk at a New York Jewish community center in December 2019, Jeffrey Goldberg, editor-in-chief of *The Atlantic*, compared Zionists immigrating to Israel to the displaced Seminoles returning to Florida, from which they were driven away by the Europeans. Goldberg also deplored the fact that Israel is losing control of "the narrative," which would reverse the "Indian and cowboys" imagery in Palestine:

But the Jews are the Indians, and the Arabs, the Palestinians, the cowboys, in the following sense. What happened in the Middle East—this is not a political commentary about what should actually be done leading to a fair and equitable solution to the challenge here—but what happened here is the equivalent of the Seminoles sitting in Oklahoma or wherever they are today, scattered around the United States—Seminoles coming together and deciding that they're going back to Florida. And going back in such numbers and telling the whites and blacks and Hispanics of Florida, Oh by the way, we're home and we'd like a state, and we'd like to take over Florida.

The people of Florida would probably say to them, you haven't been here in 200 years. This isn't your home. And the Seminoles would say, actually, it is our home. This is where our people are buried. This is the center of our religion, this is where we were expelled from.

That [discussion] doesn't happen; and people need to understand that—what's happened is, it's really interesting from an analytical perspective. As Israel has become more and more powerful as a country, and every year it becomes more powerful, it becomes bigger, it becomes more militarily powerful, economically powerful, it's lost more and more control of its own narrative. The narrative is of an indigenous people coming home to its homeland and to some degree, to a large degree, to some degree, willing to share that homeland or at least parts of that homeland with the people who moved in after. Right? But they lost total control of that narrative, because the people who were opposed to Israel's existence are very powerful and clever narrators as well.[43]

Goldberg's "cowboys and Indians" analogy posits the Palestinian people as the "cowboys," meaning the outsiders seeking to dispossess the Indigenous people. The Palestinians, as he put it, are "the people who moved in after." There is no room, in the Zionist mind, for the possibility—indeed, historical reality—that Palestine was, and remains diverse, and that just as some of the original inhabitants of that land had converted from polytheism to Judaism, with the prophet Abraham ben Terah (circa 2500 BCE) acknowledged as the "first Jew," some of these same people, either Jewish by then, or still polytheistic, later converted to Christianity. "Who did John the Baptist baptize?" is not a question he ponders. Goldberg decries the fact that Israel has lost control of "its own narrative," even though that narrative, as documented above, started out as an unapologetic European colonial narrative that acknowledges that the Palestinians have lived in Palestine "since times immemorial." In an interview for the *New Yorker* in 2006, upon the publication of his book, *Prisoners: A Story of Friendship and Terror*, in which he recounts his days as an officer in the Israeli army, during which he served as a prison guard, Goldberg speaks of his own experience there as "exotic," rather than a reconnection. "Let me not cast it as an entirely negative experience," he told his interviewer, after discussing what he described as both a "fascinating" and "troubling experience" at Ketziot prison.

It was hopelessly exotic for me. I mean, I'm from the South Shore of Long Island, and then all of a sudden I'm in the Negev Desert, by the Egyptian border, as a prison guard in what's probably the largest prison in the Middle East, guarding the future leaders of Palestine. It was pretty exciting.[44]

Another Israel advocate, Hen Mazzig, a former member of the StandWithUs Zionist propaganda outfit who specializes in infiltrating ill-informed progressive-leaning spaces, also argues that Jews from all around the world are the only Indigenous people of the land, and that Palestinians, by virtue of their claiming an Arab identity, are the invaders. Mazzig, who had served in the Israeli military as an openly gay commander, long highlighted this experience in pinkwashing ventures to show the occupying army as "tolerant." When anti-pinkwashing activists successfully argued that Israel's "gay friendliness" is little more than a smoke and mirrors propaganda tool, because a bomb is just as lethal when dropped on a family home by a straight or gay pilot, Mazzig moved on to another hasbara tactic: redwashing, or claiming indigeneity for the Zionists.[45] Interestingly, Mazzig himself is an Arab Jew, of Iraqi and Tunisian descent, but in his case, being an Arab does not make him an invader. Nor does he offer a definition of "Arab identity," an admittedly elusive concept that transcends race, ethnicity, and religion. Mazzig, like Goldberg, does not follow his own argument to its conclusion, as that conclusion would be illogical, revealing the flaw in his claim.

Mazzig is a speaker on university campuses, a contributor to many newspapers and magazines, and very active on social media. He claims on his Instagram page that all Jews—Ashkenazi, Mizrahi, and Sephardi— are indigenous to Palestine. Why then do these ethnic distinctions exist? Or rather, why is it that one can presume a "Jewish identity" that transcends ethnicity, and is based instead on shared religion and rituals, but not extend "Arab identity" to similarly diverse communities with shared language, cultural values, and geographic proximity? Palestinians would then be Arab, by virtue of identifying with Arabic culture, language, and values, but they would also be native to Palestine, rather than "invaders," as Mazzig claims us to be. In an opinion piece for the *Los Angeles Times*, he wrote that:

> Israel is a place where an indigenous people have reclaimed their land and revived their ancient language, despite being surrounded by hostile neighbors and hounded by radicalized Arab nationalists who cannot tolerate any political entity in the region other than their own.[46]

There are many problems with Mazzig's claim, not least being his argument that every single Jew is descended from the original Canaanites—that is, that no one ever converted to Judaism. But the more egregious one is his suggestion that non-Jewish Palestinians are alien to their own homeland. Thus, by stating that the Zionists have "reclaimed their land," he is implying that the land had been occupied, usurped, by the Palestinian people. In doing so, he echoes Goldberg's claim that Palestinians are the cowboys, who have displaced the Indigenous people of the land. There is no room, in either Goldberg's or Mazzig's minds, for plurality, or diversity.

In 2019, Mazzig toured several US campuses, including Vassar College, where his lecture was titled "The Indigenous Jews of the Middle East: The Forgotten Refugees." No Zionist has yet come up with a satisfactory explanation for how anyone who converts to Judaism, with no record of any ancestry in the Levant—someone like former US President Donald Trump's daughter Ivanka, who embraced the religion shortly before marrying Jared Kushner, or the white Afrikaners converting to Judaism to flee post-apartheid South Africa and move to Jewish-only colonies in the West Bank—would be "returning" to Israel. Palestinian refugees whose families can document multigenerational ties to the land, on the other hand, are considered outside conquerors since, according to Zionist redwashing, being Arab, they must have come from the Arabian Peninsula.

As the Palestinian people, in their historic homeland as well as the global diaspora, continue to resist their dispossession and disenfranchisement, the Zionist discourse had to vilify them, transform them from an Indigenous people that needed to be "spirited away" into "invaders," similar to the "merciless savages" that supposedly attacked the European settlers on the European American frontier. And as Zionists now claim that (all) Jews are the (only) Indigenous people of the ancient land of Canaan, Palestinians are denied their indigeneity, and are turned into the "cowboys" attacking the natives. Challenging the Zionist discourse in the West, along with the genderwashing of the sexual violence of settler colonialism through the foregrounding of the supposedly embracing culture of a sexually liberated Israel, remain a major task for Palestinians. But it is absolutely critical to present the question of Palestine as one of decolonization, an irrepressible impulse toward liberation and justice. It is resistance to imperialism, colonialism, and oppression, not "terrorism," nor anti-Jewish hatred.

2

Déjà Vu: Beyond Apartheid

Even as it continues to gain credence in global circles, a growing number of Palestinians remain critical of the apartheid analysis, expressing serious reservations about its usefulness. While few Palestinians would disagree with the harsh reality of state-sanctioned segregation and systemic inequality imposed upon them by Israel, critics of the apartheid framing argue that it hinges on a rights-based discourse that cannot fully encompass the complexities of the multiple Palestinian experiences. They also note the limitations it imposes on the understanding of the Palestinian struggle, as the diagnosis suggests that abolishing that specific system will end the oppression of the Palestinian people.[1] Even the Palestinian call for Boycott, Divestment, and Sanctions (BDS) has occasionally been criticized, including by some of its strong proponents—and I am one myself—for articulating a strategy that relies on international law as a framework for holding Israel accountable.

These reservations are not new. Many Palestinians have long viewed the rights-based discourse as an inadequate framework to explain and provide solutions to their plight. As Raef Zreik noted in 2004, the rights discourse "presumes the centrality of law and assumes that equal application of the law will lead to justice: the legal transcends the political and restrains it."[2] In other words, the law, like the concept of human rights, is presumed to be neutral: the flaws are not in the legal system itself, but in the fact that it is not being implemented. But, as Zreik explains, in an apartheid framework, the oppression of all Palestinians is not illegal: "At the heart of apartheid lies the concept of exclusion. But in order to exclude something, or to think of it as excluded, it is necessary first to imagine the possibility of inclusion," Zreik writes.[3] Zreik illustrates this concept of exclusion by giving the example of voting in the USA: when Black Americans are denied the right to vote in their own country, their rights are being violated, because they are being excluded from an American right. But "exclusion" does not apply in the case of French nationals who cannot vote in the USA, their rights are not violated, because they are not part of the American people. Similarly, Palestinians outside of 1948 Israel—that is, the majority of the Palestinian people—cannot in this sense be viewed as "excluded," their rights are not violated when they do not have access to the rights of Israelis. This is all the more so when there is no problematization of the idea of Israel as "the Jewish state."[4]

Meanwhile, recent reports by international human rights organizations such as Human Rights Watch which discuss Israel's impact on the entirety of the Palestinian people, describing it as apartheid "from the river to the sea," are welcome, but fall short of addressing the Palestinian people's need for sovereignty and self-determination. In other words, the recognition that Israel controls the daily life of Palestinians throughout the historic homeland is important. But most Palestinians have been exiled from that land, and Israel still controls their fate, by denying them the right of return. Additionally, many questions about Palestinians in the homeland remain unformulated and, therefore, unanswered: if Palestinians are to be given the same rights as Israelis, would they be given these rights as Israelis, or Palestinians? And what do we make of the fact that the Palestinians want to live in Palestine, not Israel? And that Palestine is more than the fragments that are recognized in hegemonic discourse as "illegally occupied," it is the ancestral homeland, from the river to the sea. Would a US-based refugee whose parents were expelled from Haifa have to live as an Israeli, if she were to finally be able to return home? And would she be allowed to return to her family's home—an acknowledgment of the Palestinian people's collective rights, that would supersede an Israeli citizen's individual rights? Can the human rights discourse be sufficiently "reformed" to allow for justice, or should oppressed communities look at an alternative system? "Reforming" Israel to make it a truly democratic and diverse country would abolish it as the Jewish state, which is how it defines itself.

Land Back

Looking specifically at post-apartheid South Africa, and post-Civil Rights Act USA, Noura Erakat writes that:

> the achievement of human rights amounted to the removal of obstacles for blacks without implementing re-distributive policies and rehabilitative measures such as reparations aimed at creating a more just society. Moreover, the wealth and privilege of whites, built upon, and facilitated by, slave and indentured labor, remained intact, as doing otherwise would have violated the human rights of the white populations under existing applications of the law. Thus, the triumph of human rights does not necessarily lead to justice.[5]

Clearly, the importance of discussing Palestine as a decolonial struggle and an anti-apartheid struggle cannot be over-emphasized. And the most distinguishing characteristic of settler colonialism is that it is land theft. As such, decolonization in a settler colonial context simply cannot be achieved without land restitution. Decolonization is not an abstract concept, "it is not a metaphor," as Eve Tuck and K. Wayne Yang argue.[6] Instead, as they write, decolonization, "as a process, would repatriate land to Indigenous peoples,"[7] and "Decolonizing the Americas means all land is repatriated and all settlers become landless."[8] Indeed, from Turtle Island to Palestine, decolonization can only be achieved once the formerly colonized have full sovereignty over the entire land of which they were forcefully dispossessed. If South Africa is to serve as a model, as indeed it should, it must also serve as a cautionary tale: the official end of legal apartheid barely improved the living circumstances of Black Africans, who remain impoverished, living in dismal shanty towns, in "townships" and informal housing throughout the country, with little access to higher quality schools, or health care. Most work multiple jobs and still cannot make ends meet. As Loubna Qutami writes in an article based on a Palestine Youth Movement fact-finding delegation to South Africa that she participated in, the most profound lesson the delegates learned is that "if solutions do not allow for a complete redistribution of land, wealth and power there will be no true Palestinian liberation."[9]

In South Africa today, the extreme poverty, compounding the long-established pattern of "masculinity" being equated with control over women, aggravates gender-based violence (GBV), with that country frequently described as "the rape capital of the world" and annually ranking among the world's most dangerous countries for women.[10] The crisis of GBV in South Africa can be related to the fact that the end of apartheid there was not accompanied with an intentional effort to return the stolen land to its rightful stewards. As we will see in Chapter 3, the macro level of oppression trickles down onto the domestic or micro level, with poverty, unemployment, dispossession, and overall disenfranchisement and lack of opportunities translating into greater levels of GBV, mostly perpetuated by men against women, children, and gender non-conforming individuals. As we look at the multigenerational impact of disenfranchisement and poverty, it is important to note the specific ways Black women were discriminated against in apartheid South Africa. For example, if a woman's husband died, she would be evicted from her house, as Black women did not have property rights until 1988. Today, decades after the official end of apartheid in that country, the ongoing economic inequality and gentrification continue to push Black South Africans away from the cities into the crowded townships, where they have even fewer opportunities to advance socially. The traumatized survivors of GBV, mostly women, girls, and gender non-conforming individuals, also have difficulty securing better jobs, and many continue to have no options but to stay in physically, psychologically, and economically abusive relationships.[11]

In 2020, the World Bank deemed South Africa the world's most unequal society, estimating that the top 10 percent owned 71 percent of the nation's assets. The split is still largely along racial lines; the bottom 60 percent, largely comprising blacks and "colored" (multiracial individuals and Asians descended from the era of slavery and colonial rule), controls 7 percent of the country's net wealth. Half the population lives on less than five dollars a day.[12] Gender-based violence is systemic and, under the COVID-19 lockdown, has been called South Africa's second pandemic: survivors trapped at home with their abusers. It is thus incumbent on Palestinians to organize now, for a healthier post-Zionist society, where *all* can thrive, even as we continue to learn from and support our sisters in South Africa, Turtle Island, and wherever colonialism has devastated the indigenous communities. To quote Qutami again:

> delegates articulated two important lessons. First, to break cycles of gendered violence in the struggle for political liberation, institutions must mandate trauma-informed approaches to social healing as integral to, not at the periphery of, the liberation movement. It is important to build popular grassroots movements that account for women's liberation as part of national liberation, but which also reject colonial, Orientalist and imperial feminist discourses that have become especially prevalent in the funding criteria for non-governmental organizations in Palestine since the beginning of the so-called war on terror. A second lesson follows that if Palestinians are to achieve true liberation, political movements must implement models of accountability and justice at every level of struggle. For example, the Tal3at Movement is using grassroots approaches to make ending violence against women and national liberation inseparable.[13]

Gendered violence is so much part and parcel of colonialism that it permeates all societies, not just the colonized. In the USA, for example, Indigenous women have been most disproportionally the victims of gendered violence from the early days of European conquest to the present. Today, Alaska, the state with the largest Indigenous population, is the deadliest state in the USA for women, with more than 50 percent of Alaska Native women reporting violent sexual assault and rape. But all American women are subject to unfathomable misogyny, as evidenced in the Supreme Court's June 2022 decision to overturn *Roe v. Wade*, the 1973 landmark ruling that had established the constitutional right to abortion. And the fact that Americans elect or appoint, time and again, men accused of sexual assault and rape to some of the highest positions in the country, offers no reassurance that this is likely to be addressed and redressed soon. Similarly, domestic violence pervades all communities in Israel, aggravated by the militarization of Israeli society, which normalizes violence within the home, as well as the fact that Orthodox Jewish communities are deeply patriarchal. While the national crisis was mostly hushed until the COVID-19 pandemic, it is now being addressed at the official level, as reports of GBV rose by close to 300 percent during the lockdown, leading many Israeli advocates to say the home should not be more dangerous than the outdoors.

Many historic reasons account for the inequality that plagues South Africa today. These include unemployment, an educational system in shambles, and a collapsing public health system. But as one report makes clear, "the largest dividing line is land, where the legacy of apartheid meets the failures and broken promises of the current government. It's manifested most plainly in the lack of affordable housing, particularly in urban areas."[14] The number of decaying slums which Blacks relocate to out of extreme poverty has gone from 300 in 1994, when apartheid was officially abolished, to 2,700 in 2019. Again, as we consider the global feminization of poverty, we need to account for how this phenomenon will impact post-apartheid Palestinian society, especially taking into consideration Israel's maiming, disabling, and killing of Palestinian boys and men, who depend on women's unpaid labor of sustenance and care, and their underpaid work outside the house. Nor does the intensification of lethal masculinity and patriarchy in Palestinian society, as evidenced by the alarming rise in femicides, portend a bright future for Palestinian women, unless it is addressed as part of the nexus of disenfranchisement, rather than an afterthought. History has taught us again and again that other oppressions do not end *after* national liberation," unless they are addressed as part of the liberation struggle.

Definitions Matter

Even as we insist that the Palestinian struggle is a decolonial struggle, the apartheid framework should not be dismissed, and has its very significant merits. Exposing and denouncing Israel's legal system as one of apartheid has changed the global discourse about that country and catalyzed a new generation of activists. The historical model of apartheid South Africa, correctly viewed as one of grievous injustice that was overcome in part thanks to global solidarity, is inspiring. And as evidenced from the many reports being issued today, Israel is no longer viewed as merely an "occupying country," but as an apartheid state. This recognition was reflected in the USA, for example, when the largest coalition of activist groups advocating for justice in Palestine officially announced, at its October 2016 annual conference, that it was changing its name from the US Campaign to End the Israeli Occupation, to the US Campaign for Palestinian Rights. Yet, the choice of the word "rights" is itself revealing of the dominant framework for organizing and advocacy in the USA.

Meanwhile, Israel apologists persist that Israel is not engaging in apartheid. Similarly, even Palestinian Authority President Mahmoud Abbas, in his typical behind the curve mode, only uses the apartheid language as a warning to Israel that it will *become* guilty of apartheid if it does not agree to some Palestinian demands. (Abbas' term expired in 2009, but he remains in office, against the wishes of most Palestinians, because he is such a good servant to Israel). Yet, the definition of apartheid is quite clear. Specifically, Article II of the 1976 United Nations International Convention on the Suppression and Punishment of the Crime of Apartheid defines it as:

For the purpose of the present Convention, the term "the crime of apartheid", which shall include similar policies and racial segregation and discrimination as practiced in southern Africa, shall apply to the following inhumane acts committed for the purpose of establishing and maintaining domination by one racial group of persons over any other racial group of persons and systematically oppressing them:

a. Denial to a member or members of a racial group or groups of the right to life and liberty of person

i. By murder of members of a racial group or groups;

ii. By the infliction upon the members of a racial group or groups of serious bodily or mental harm, by the infringement of their freedom or dignity, or by subjecting them to torture or to cruel, inhuman or degrading treatment or punishment;

iii. By arbitrary arrest and illegal imprisonment of the members of a racial group or groups;

b. Deliberate imposition on a racial group or groups of living conditions calculated to cause its or their physical destruction in whole or in part;

c. Any legislative measures and other measures calculated to prevent a racial group or groups from participation in the political, social, economic and cultural life of the country and the deliberate creation of conditions preventing the full development of such a group or groups, in particular by denying to members of a racial group or groups basic human rights and freedoms, including the right to work, the right to form recognized trade unions, the right to education, the right to leave and to return to their country, the right to a nationality, the right to freedom of movement and residence, the right to freedom of opinion and expression, and the right to freedom of peaceful assembly, and association;

d. Any measures including legislative measures, designed to divide the population along racial lines by the creation of separate reserves and ghettos for the members of a racial group or groups, the prohibition of mixed marriages among members of various racial groups, the expropriation of landed property belonging to a racial group or groups or to members thereof;

e. Exploitation of the labour of the members of a racial group or groups, in particular by submitting them to forced labour;

f. Persecution of organizations and persons, by depriving them of fundamental rights and freedoms, because they oppose apartheid.[15]

In turn, "racial discrimination" is defined thus:

According to the United Nations Convention on the Elimination of All Forms of Racial Discrimination, the term "racial discrimination" shall mean any distinction, exclusion, restriction or preference based on race, colour, descent, or national or ethnic which has the purpose or effect of nullifying or impairing the recognition, enjoyment or exercise, on an equal footing, of human rights and fundamental freedoms in the political, economic, social, cultural or any other field of public life.[16]

The official definition of "racial discrimination" is important, insofar as some will defend Israel against the charge by arguing that "Jewishness" is not a race, but a religion, a "descent," and/or an ethnicity—all of which are also included in the United Nations definition of "racial discrimination." There is one other official, legal definition of "apartheid," provided by the 2002 Rome Statute of the International Criminal Court:

The "crime of apartheid" means inhumane acts of a character similar to those referred to in paragraph 1, committed in the context of an institutionalised regime of systematic oppression and domination by one racial group over any other racial group or groups and committed with the intention of maintaining that regime.[17]

"Paragraph 1" in the definition above refers to "any of the following acts when committed as part of a widespread or systematic attack directed against any civilian population, with knowledge of the attack." As Israel systematically denies millions of exiled Palestinians the right to return to their homeland, restricts the freedom of movement of nearly 3 million people with over five hundred checkpoints and other roadblocks in the West Bank, imprisons thousands of civilians without charges, and has held another 2 million Palestinians prisoner in the Gaza Strip for over fourteen years, it is an act of bad faith to deny that Israel is actively and knowingly engaging in the crime of apartheid.

Cosmetic Differences

It cannot be over-emphasized that differences between Israeli and apartheid South African practices do not determine whether the oppressive system in Israel constitutes apartheid or not—the definition of that crime should determine that. Yet, opponents of the apartheid framing maintain that the Israeli state is a "democracy," in which, unfortunately, a handful of extremist politicians hold sway. They claim that those Israeli politicians are the problem, and not the Zionist system itself. In other words, they would argue for the reform of Zionism, rather than the abolition of the Zionist state. They are displaying, with regards to Israel, the kind of myopia and short-term memory that Americans display, when they blame former President Trump for the wave of white supremacy engulfing the country, ignoring the fact that he merely rode a resurgence of the racial hatred that has always existed—indeed, that is at the very foundation of this country.

Similarly, Israel apologists point to Benjamin Netanyahu's long tenure as the problem, and the reason Israeli society is more openly violent and hate-filled today. They do not see in the former prime minister the outward expression of the country's ethos, a country which repeatedly re-elected an avowed separatist and supremacist. Netanyahu's successor, Naftali Bennett, is himself a first-generation Israeli (his parents moved from San Francisco to Haifa in 1967), an ultranationalist, and champion of the settler movement. But whereas the settler movement is frequently criticized, Zionists conveniently forget that the perpetrators of al-Nakba were also settlers, who moved into Palestinian homes in 1948. The majority of the Palestinian people were displaced in 1948 and have never been allowed to return to their homes and villages since that year, not just since Netanyahu first rose to the leadership of Israel in 1996. Golda Meir denied our existence in 1969, and Jabotinsky elaborated on how our attachment to our land is to be utterly violated in 1923, as he was formulating his vision for the future Jewish state. Palestinians in Israel were subjected to drastic military law, unlike their Jewish compatriots who enjoyed civilian law, from 1948 to 1966—a legal distinction between communities based on religion and national origin. This unequal treatment is foundational to Zionism, not a later departure from a previously righteous path. Simply, just as the USA would not have come into existence without white supremacy, Israel is the reification of Jewish supremacy over Palestinians.

All Palestinians who live in historic Palestine today, from the river to the sea, are living under Israel's control, and do not have equal rights with Jewish Israelis. Our 1948 catastrophe—the violent privileging of one (perceived) race over another—started long before "the occupation," generally dated post June 1967. Shira Robinson's *Citizen Strangers: Palestinians and the Birth of Israel's Liberal Settler State* provides a detailed analysis of Israel's founding and the early years of the state, whose first prime minister, David Ben-Gurion, had determined that it must have an 80 percent Jewish majority.[18] Consequently, those Palestinians who were not exiled during al-Nakba, an estimated 20 percent of the Palestinian people, amounting to approximately 15 percent of Israel's population in 1948, were subjected to draconian military law, while the displaced Palestinians who attempted to return were shot on sight, in what Robinson termed a "war on return" that preceded, by some seventy years, the shooting at refugees in the "Great March of Return," which began in the Gaza Strip in March 2018.

Apartheid is an evolving system of practices that responds to developments on the ground. Israel is constantly legislating new restrictions on Palestinians that it says are temporary or emergency measures, which it nevertheless keeps renewing indefinitely. Because these measures are theoretically "temporary," Zionists will claim that they are not "law," and that therefore Israel is not engaging in apartheid but responding to crises. It should be noted that the 1967 occupation was also meant to be temporary, while Israel has since been busy establishing "facts on the ground" that make it clear it is fully intent on keeping control over the entirety of historic Palestine. Only recently have Israeli politicians become honest about their determination to annex all of historic Palestine.

One example of a law that was supposed to be "temporary" when it was first passed in 2003, but which has since been extended annually, is the "Citizenship and Entry into Israel Law." This law, which evokes the American "Muslim Ban," prevents Israeli citizens from bringing their spouses into Israel if those spouses are from Iran, Afghanistan, Lebanon, Libya, Sudan, Syria, Iraq, Pakistan, Yemen, and the "Occupied Palestinian Territories." Obviously, these banned spouses are not Jewish, as the latter would not need to be married to an Israeli to reside in Israel—the "Citizenship and Entry into Israel Law" thus impacts Israel's Palestinian families, not its Jewish ones. Palestinian who remained in what became Israel after 1948 are citizens, but not nationals, another legal distinction which will be further discussed.

Anecdotal comparisons to South Africa illustrate the blind spot of most Israel apologists who believe themselves "liberal," while clearly incapable of seeing the oppression Israel engages in. During the First Intifada, I was a doctoral student at a major research university in the USA. I was gathering signatures for a petition condemning Israel's forced closures of Palestinian schools, and asked a member of my cohort if he would sign. This student, a white South African, did not seem sufficiently knowledgeable about the situation, and I thought the best way to explain Israel's oppression of the Palestinians to him would be by making the comparison to South Africa. He refused to sign, saying: "So you're telling me that the Palestinians are the equivalent of the blacks in South Africa. Well let *me* tell you something: the problem in South Africa is the blacks." Many years later, I was eating at a restaurant and overheard the conversation between two older white women seated at a table close to me. One spoke with a North American accent, the other with what I soon understood was a South African accent. The American woman asked her friend: "How long has it been since you went home? Do you miss South Africa?" The other responded, dreamily: "Do I miss it? Heaven. South Africa was heaven on earth. But they ruined it..." I looked very intently in their direction, hoping they'd ask me what the matter was, and I would have blurted out, "Heaven for whom? Was it heaven for the dispossessed oppressed Black South Africans? And who exactly ruined it?" But they didn't look my way. The white South African woman was too absorbed in her nostalgic recollections of the "heavenly" days of apartheid. I remained quiet, ruminating over the thought that just as this white woman believed South Africa was "ruined" with the end of apartheid, so Zionists believe Israel would be "ruined" if it gave equal rights to all its citizens.

Not all white South Africans are afflicted with such myopia about their country's shortcomings. Jennifer Davis, a white South African anti-apartheid activist who had to flee her country in the 1960s, tells a story she found very eye-opening. "An early encounter taught me a keen lesson in the tunnel vision many Americans use to perceive themselves and their society," Davis recalls.[19]

A few weeks after we arrived [from South Africa to New York] we were invited to dinner by friends of my parents, wealthy professionals they had met at international conferences. They lived in a beautiful townhouse with magnificent artwork on the walls. They were genuinely kind to me, and concerned about how we were settling in...

After dinner one of the guests said to me "You must see great differences between South Africa and here." Well of course I did, but I also saw great similarities. So I said, "Yes, but I also see a tremendous number of very poor black people, and wealthy people seem mostly white." Slightly disconcerted, she pulled herself up to her elegant height and said "There are no poor people in America."[20]

Davis explains that:

I've told that story often to the groups of people concerned about apartheid and poverty in Africa who kept asking me why many whites in South Africa seemed blind to the destruction inflicted on black society by apartheid. This was a useful learning experience for subsequent political organizing.[21]

Just as many whites in South Africa seemed blind to the destruction inflicted on Black society, so, today, many Zionists seem blind to the oppression of Palestinians by the country they love and support. To millions of Zionists today, the problem in Israel is the Palestinians...

Some Key Differences

Apologists for Israel often cite the major differences between Israel and South Africa in order to refute the apartheid label. These are around labor, citizenship, and the right to vote. These differences deserve a lengthy discussion, which I will structure around their impact on the disenfranchised communities, rather than on the "legal system."

Labor

White South Africans relied heavily on the labor of Black South Africans, whereas the early Zionists consciously sought to only employ Jews, especially in manual labor, as they aspired to build a Jewish society, with a Jewish working class. The political decision to have Jewish immigrants work the land came in part from a desire to create a physical bond with the new country, whose soil was otherwise foreign to the European people now claiming it as their own. Another motive was the desire to counter centuries of being denied the right to own land in various European countries, because of anti-Jewish laws there. Europe's Jews were also forbidden from joining most trade guilds, a ban which pushed them into a small handful of professions, such as seamstresses, market-peddlers, and tailoring. But by far the most common professions available to Jews in the Middle Ages centered on money transactions: tax collection, pawnbrokers, and usury. Many Jews in medieval Europe were compelled into making a living as usurers by the Christian authorities, who considered the practice a sin, and forced it onto non-Christians—an unfortunate situation which rendered Jews in these occupations even more unpopular among their compatriots. While many trade and guild restrictions eased during the Enlightenment, anti-Jewish sentiment remained virulent over the centuries. Essayists such as Voltaire and Diderot pilloried Jews in their writing, and sixteenth-century Protestant reformist Martin Luther, the most widely read thinker in his time, produced plentiful anti-Jewish rhetoric that later underpinned Nazi ideology in the early twentieth century. Modern Christian Europe's hatred of Jews frequently reverted back to old forms of abuse. Thus, the yellow star that Jews had to wear during the Third Reich harks back to the twelfth century, while ghettoes, which began in the Middle Ages, continued into the nineteenth and early twentieth century. In the modern, "redemptive" Israel, Jews were finally able to work any trade they wanted, but also, they could now farm the land and sell the product of their own manual labor—even if their land owner-ship had come through horrific means, namely, the ethnic cleansing of its rightful owners.

But Israel needed the skills of the Palestinians, even in the kibbutzim of the 1940s, 1950s, and 1960s. Andrew Ross's award-winning *Stone Men: The Palestinians Who Built Israel* is a wonderful exposé of the myth of Zionist labor from the early days of the kibbutzim to the present.[22] In the 1960s and 1970s, Palestinians residing in the Gaza Strip contrib-uted to building Israel to a much greater degree than is usually acknowl-edged, leading to the common statement "we build their houses while they demolish ours."[23] In the 1990s, Israel "rectified" its dependence up until that time on Palestinian workers by facilitating the official, large-scale employment of foreign workers. However, even with the presence of a foreign workforce, many jobs continued to be dominated by Pal-estinian labor—especially in construction, and in the settlements. The trend of employing Palestinians for the hard manual labor remained until a temporary migrant worker policy was introduced in 1991, which brought several hundred thousand workers from Asia, Africa, and South America to replace Palestinian labor. Specifically, the Foreign Workers Law postulates that work permits would be granted for foreign workers in nursing care, agriculture, construction, welding and industrial profes-sions, hotel work, and "ethnic" cuisine.[24]

Overall, the foreign workers toil at the same physical labor the Pal-estinians used to provide for Israelis, and frequently suffer worse con-ditions. Many have paid upwards of $10,000 for visas to work in Israel, they are required to surrender their passport to their employers, and if they are sponsored by these employers, they cannot change jobs, no matter how abusive or exploitative their circumstances. Today, two-thirds of the foreign workers in Israel are women, and two-thirds are there illegally. Of these, most have overstayed their legal employment period, making them more vulnerable to abuse by their employers. They are also paid less than the Palestinians used to earn, with no benefits. A 2002 study shows that over 80 percent of male foreign workers in Israel were paid less than minimum wage.[25] According to Israel Drori, author of *Foreign Workers in Israel*: "What began as a political corrective—avoiding the danger of hiring Palestinians to do work that Jewish Israelis would not—has developed into a social and economic problem the state does not know how to handle."[26] Notice that Drori speaks of a need to "correct" the employment of Palestinians, clearly viewed as a politically dangerous practice. In their 2003 report, "Foreign Workers in Israel: A Contemporary Form of Slavery," Michael Ellman and Smain Laacher also note that Israel intentionally brought in foreign workers to replace Palestinian labor.

The drastic economic downturn in the Gaza Strip in 1991 reveals the magnitude of Israel's reliance on Palestinian labor before the introduction of the Foreign Workers Law: within just one year, from 1990 to 1991, the number of Palestinian families receiving food aid rose from 10,000 to 120,000, as most Palestinians lost their source of income from employment within Israel. These figures pre-date the blockade which Israel imposed in 2007. Today, unemployment in Gaza is the highest in the world, according to separate reports by the World Bank and the International Labour Organization, standing at over 50 percent of the total population, with over 68 percent of women unemployed.[27] Actual unemployment may be much higher, as these figures do not account for people who have given up on looking for work, due to the unavailability of employment in the strip. Over 80 percent of people in Gaza are fully dependent on aid for their subsistence.[28]

Meanwhile, foreign workers, mostly women from the Philippines, Sri Lanka, and Nepal, are primarily domestic maids, and in-home caregivers for the sick and elderly. An increasing number of men from China, Thailand, and Nigeria have also been employed in construction since the early 2000s, when they were first brought in to replace Palestinian laborers during the Second Intifada. The rise in foreign workers is simultaneous with the overall rise in sex trafficking and exploitation of sex workers. Israel is a destination country for human trafficking, with many women from Eastern Europe (primarily Russia, Ukraine, Moldova, Uzbekistan, and Belarus), as well as China, being trafficked to Israel for forced sex work, often by organized crime groups. Despite stringent employment rules set out by the Israeli government, about two-thirds of foreign workers in Israel are working without a permit, and receiving no benefits. Israelis apparently prefer that to employing Palestinians.[29]

But regardless of the extent to which Israel replaces Palestinian labor with foreign workers, the use of Indigenous versus imported labor is not part of the definition of apartheid. Systematic oppression "for the purpose of establishing and maintaining domination by one racial group of persons over any other racial group of persons" is part of that definition, and domination in Israel necessitated "correcting" its dependence on Palestinian labor. This domination has significantly aggravated the feminization of poverty, and overall sexual exploitation.

Citizenship

Critics of the apartheid language also argue that apartheid was the legal system in South Africa, but is not encoded in the Israeli constitution. This claim can be refuted on many levels. First and foremost, Israel does not have a formal, written constitution, and relies instead on "Basic Laws," which were initially intended to serve as a draft of the constitution. This constitution, however, has been postponed since 1950. The Basic Laws theoretically grant all citizens equal rights and can only be amended by a supermajority. However, there is no Basic Law defining Israeli citizenship. Instead, the Citizenship Act, which determines who can claim Israeli citizenship, maintains a crucial distinction between the categories of citizenship (Hebrew "ezrahut," Arabic "muatana") and nationality (Hebrew "le'om," Arabic "jinsiyya"). Both Israeli Jews and those Palestinians born within the 1948 borders are "citizens" of Israel, with the Palestinians making up just over 20 percent of Israel's total population. Israeli citizenship then bifurcates into different "nationalities," the most important ones being Jewish, Arab, and Druze. Thus, there is no "Israeli nationality," instead, there is Jewish or Arab nationality, determined by religion, and "Israeli citizenship."

Many Israeli laws explicitly or implicitly discriminate based on "nationality," in effect privileging Jewish citizens and disadvantaging the non-Jewish citizens of the state. Foremost among these is the Law of Return, first passed in 1950, which grants any individual, anywhere in the world, with one Jewish grandmother, the right to live in Israel and claim Israeli citizenship immediately upon arrival. The Law of Return was amended in 1970 to include granting citizenship to a "child and a grandchild of a Jew, the spouse of a Jew, the spouse of a child of a Jew and the spouse of a grandchild of a Jew."[30] These privileges, however, are not given to the child, or spouse of a non-Jewish Israeli citizen, thus further disenfranchising Palestinian citizens of Israel.

Israel's *Law* of Return is in stark contrast to the internationally recognized universal *Right* of Return, which states that Palestinian refugees should be allowed to return to their homeland and be compensated for losses incurred during their forced displacement. The Right of Return was first formulated by United Nations negotiator Folke Bernadotte in June 1948, immediately after the onset of al-Nakba. It was formally recognized by the United Nations as an inalienable human right in the 1948 Universal Declaration of Human Rights, (UN 217A), Article 13, which states: "a. Everyone has the right to freedom of movement and residence within the borders of each State. b. Everyone has the right to leave any country, including his own, and to return to his country."[31] The Right of Return was further confirmed, also in December 1948, in UN Resolution 194, which:

> Resolves that the refugees wishing to return to their homes and live at peace with their neighbours should be permitted to do so at the earliest practicable date, and that compensation should be paid for the property of those choosing not to return and for loss of or damage to property which, under principles of international law or in equity, should be made good by the Governments or authorities responsible.[32]

Yet, Israel has been in violation of this internationally recognized "inalienable" universal human right since 1948, even as it implements its own "Law of Return" for Jews only. Consequently, the Palestinian refugee problem is the longest-lived refugee problem in modern history, and until Russia's 2022 war on Ukraine, made up approximately

40 percent of the world's refugees, despite the relatively small size of the country.

Another discriminatory law is the Ban on Family Unification, which prohibits an Israeli citizen from bringing a spouse from the Occupied Territories (West Bank and Gaza Strip, but not the Jewish settlements in the West Bank) or Iran, Lebanon, Syria, and Iraq. Again, this ban effectively impacts Palestinian but not Jewish citizens of Israel. There are also temporary measures regarding security, land, political representation in the Knesset, education, and culture, which also explicitly privilege Jewish nationals. Uri Davis' excellent 1987 study, *Israel: An Apartheid State*,[33] as well as Ben White's 2009 *Israeli Apartheid: A Beginner's Guide*,[34] both analyze Israel's legal and para-legal measures disenfranchising non-Jewish citizens. Both books were written before the Nation State Bill, a new "Basic Law" passed in 2018, which was immediately met with worldwide condemnation for legislating these multiple discriminatory practices.[35] Feminists of color point to these discriminatory laws that impact families as one of the many reasons that abolishing the Zionist system is a feminist issue. Meanwhile, Palestinians in the West Bank do not have Israeli citizenship, even though just about every aspect of their lives is controlled by Israel.

Voting and Political Representation

Blacks could not vote in apartheid South Africa, whereas Palestinian citizens of Israel, estimated to number 1,890,000 in 2019, can, and most do. Yet, there are 8 million Palestinians directly under Israeli control in the West Bank and Gaza Strip, who cannot vote in the elections that determine every aspect of their lives. Opponents of the apartheid analysis will argue that Israel only controls the West Bank for "security reasons," leaving administrative matters to the Palestinian Authority, and that it no longer occupies the Gaza Strip, which is ruled by Hamas. Yet, a preponderance of evidence illustrates that Israel has control over the entire Palestinian people within historic Palestine. There are over five hundred Israeli checkpoints and other roadblocks in the West Bank, restricting Palestinian movement. Visitors from outside the country need to obtain permission from Israel to visit the West Bank. As for the Gaza Strip, it is not Hamas, but rather Israel, who is imposing a quasi-genocidal siege there on the 2 million impoverished Palestinians, 70 percent of whom are refugees from other towns and cities in historic Palestine. It is Israel that shoots at fishermen who go beyond the nautical mileage within which Israel arbitrarily determines residents of Gaza can fish. (Under the Oslo Agreement, Gaza fishermen can go out twenty nautical miles from shore. Israel immediately restricted that to twelve miles, and often arbitrarily reduces this distance to under three miles.) And it is Israel that is at the root of the electricity and water crisis in Gaza, as it has repeatedly bombed Gaza's power plant and water infrastructure, and refuses to allow repair materials into the Gaza Strip. The chronic electricity crisis in the region brings any semblance of normalcy to a stop, and the water crisis is threatening people's very lives.

So the difference in voting rights between apartheid South Africa and present-day Israel is more accurately reformulated as "No Black African could vote during the apartheid era, whereas a small minority of the Palestinian people, namely those who are citizens of Israel, can vote today." Yet, Israel has control over the entire Palestinian people within historic Palestine. Additionally, by denying the 7 million Palestinian refugees in the global diaspora their Right of Return, Israel is also determining various aspects of the lives of these Palestinians too. Of all Palestinians impacted by Israel, only those within Israel's 1948 borders, an approximate 14 percent of the entire Palestinian population, estimated at 14 million globally, can vote. And this minority must vote for "representatives" who have endorsed Zionism, in accordance with the 1958 Knesset Basic Law which states that:

A candidates' list shall not participate in elections to the Knesset, and a person shall not be a candidate for election to the Knesset, if the objects or actions or the actions of the person, expressly or by implication, include one of the following:

1. negation of the existence of the State of Israel as a Jewish and democratic state;

2. incitement to racism;

3. support of armed struggle, by a hostile state or a terrorist organization, against the State of Israel.[36]

Despite the Basic Law above, which would disqualify candidates who question whether it is possible that Israel can be simultaneously Jewish and democratic, there have been Palestinian members of the Israeli Knesset since it was first formed. Again, this is different from the case of Blacks in South Africa, who could not serve in their country's apartheid government. As for the ban against "incitement to racism," it is clearly overlooked when that racism is directed at Palestinians.

Historically, a disproportionate number of the Arab members of Knesset have been from the Druze community, who occupy a unique and complex position in Israel, where they are considered "Arab" but placed in a category different from the rest of the Palestinians who lived in historic Palestine. Numbering a mere 120,000, the Druze account for approximately 1.6 percent of the population of Israel. Like all Palestinians who stayed on after the founding of Israel, the Druze are routinely denied building permits by Israel, lack basic infrastructure in their existing towns and villages, and are regularly fined for undertaking "illegal construction" on their homes that is necessary to accommodate the natural growth of their families and communities. Druze leaders signed what they describe as "a covenant of blood" with Israel in 1956 and requested that their community be designated as a separate ethnic community in 1957. They are the only non-Jewish community that is drafted into the Israeli army, the Israel Defense Forces, where, because they speak Arabic, they often serve at military checkpoints and other points of friction with Palestinians—a practice that further fragments the Palestinian people, as it fosters hostility between Druze and other Palestinians.[37] Up to 87 percent of Druze men serve in the army, where they have a higher percentage of officers and combat unit soldiers than male Jewish conscripts, while Druze women have the option of volunteering for National Service instead, with the vast majority electing for that.[38] Not coincidentally, the Druze are also disproportionately represented in those rare instances when the Israeli army finds one of its own guilty of "unnecessary violence." There is a further distinction between

Druze Israelis from within Israel's 1948 borders, and the Druze who live in the Golan Heights, the territory which Israel conquered from Syria in 1967 and has been occupying ever since. The Druze in the Golan Heights have refused Israeli citizenship, and identify as Syrian, although they hold "permanent Israeli residency." The distinction between "Druze" and "Palestinian" is an important one to keep in mind when one is otherwise looking at statistics for "Arabs" in Israel, as both communities are routinely lumped together, despite significant political differences.

In 2019, there were 14 Arabs serving in the 120-member Knesset, 3 of whom Druze. Various restrictions on the political opinions of these Knesset members (MKs) ensure that they follow the Zionist line, failing which they can lose their seat. For example, legislation passed in 2016 stipulates that a member of the Knesset can be suspended if 90 out of 120 MKs find their ideas to be "inappropriate." Among MKs who have thus been suspended, for periods of between two and four months, are Haneen Zoabi, Basel Ghattas, and Jamal Zahalka, who intervened in 2016 to have the Israeli government return to their families the bodies of Palestinians killed in fighting. This legislation against "inappropriate ideas" and behavior allows for elected officials to be deprived of their parliamentary rights not because they have broken any law, but because their political agenda is found to be unacceptable. While "suspended," an MK cannot vote on any legislation, nor serve on committees—which is where all legislation originates, until these privileges are reinstated. Right-wing Likud Knesset member Sharren Haskel justified the stripping of these MKs' rights by claiming: "No one should be able to use their parliamentary privilege to destroy our democracy."[39]

Long-standing state-sanctioned discrimination was eventually enshrined into a new Basic Law in 2018, with the "Nation State Law" which explicitly restricts the right to self-determination to Jews, as it names Israel "the Nation-State of the Jewish People." Then Prime Minister Netanyahu applauded the passage of the law as "a pivotal moment in the annals of Zionism and the State of Israel." "We enshrined in law the basic principle of our existence," Netanyahu told the Knesset, adding,

This is our state—the Jewish state. In recent years, there have been some who have attempted to put this in doubt, to undercut the core of our being. Today, we made it law: This is our nation, language, and flag.[40]

Likud Knesset Member Avi Dichter, who sponsored the law, said:

Ever since I began promoting the law, I was told that it was obvious, but the remarks of the [opposition, predominantly Palestinian] Joint List could not be missed: "We will win—we were here before you, and we will be here after you." This law is the clearest answer to those who think this way.[41]

Among its many articles, the Jewish Nation State law demoted Arabic from the country's second official language to a language with an otherwise undefined "special status." It names Jerusalem, illegally annexed and occupied, as the capital of Israel, and encourages the promotion and establishment of segregated Jewish settlements. Adalah, the Legal Center for Minority Rights in Israel, said the following about the law:

The law is not merely declarative or a confirmation of the status quo ante: while the state's policy of discrimination against Palestinians has existed since 1948, there is a major difference between discriminatory practices and the codification of these policies in a new Basic Law with constitutional status. The law lends discriminatory policies against Palestinians greater legitimacy and *requires* the executive, judiciary, and other authorities to implement them under the rule of law. The law also reduces the very grounds on which such discrimination can be challenged under Israeli law.[42]

Whataboutism, Then and Now

Palestine rights activists, particularly those who look to South Africa as a model, often forget that the struggle there was met with similar attempts to deflect attention from South Africa by pointing the finger at other countries. This phenomenon, known as "whataboutism" in activist circles, is common today when people complain about organizers "singling out" Israel for criticism. What about Syria, where the viciousness of Bashar Assad's war on his own people eclipses Israel's treatment of the Palestinians in the West Bank? What about Yemen, where a Saudi-led coalition has intensified a civil war resulting in famine that threatens over 20 million people, more than half the population, after a popular rebellion against the authoritarian president? It is sad indeed that Israel should compare itself to some of the world's greatest offenders in order to look "better." As a self-proclaimed democracy, a beacon of modernity and civilization, shouldn't Israel be comparing itself to the best, rather than to notorious authoritarian regimes and monarchies? And always, always, we get "what about Hamas?" "Hamas would kill you if you were outed as gay in the Gaza Strip," the Israel apologists gloat. Their comparisons are to despots, their "whataboutism" trump card is gender, and gay rights.

Those supporters of Israel clearly ignore the fact that the majority of Palestine rights activists do not have tunnel-vision, single-issue agendas, and that we also support women's and queer rights in Saudi Arabia, Iran, Palestine, as well as the USA. In fact, we are the ones asking Zionists how they can support women's rights in the USA, Saudi Arabia, and Iran, but not those of Palestinians in Israel. But beyond the current unjustified charge of "singling out Israel," it is helpful to know that there was a very similar attempt at "whataboutism" during the South African anti-apartheid struggle, aimed at sidetracking global outrage at South Africa's treatment of non-whites, by pointing out the fact that the neighboring countries were not blameless. A 1989 article by Anne-Marie Kriek in the *Christian Science Monitor* defends South Africa by showing how regressive other African countries are.[43] Kriek, at the time, was a lecturer in international politics at the University of South Africa, and wrote her article while on sabbatical in Ft. Collins, Colorado, where she was appalled at American support for the anti-apartheid struggle. The article is striking in how it parallels today's Zionist arguments in defense of Israel. "While the violation of human rights is the norm rather than the exception in most of Africa's 42 black-ruled states, the spotlight remains on South Africa," the article opens, before delivering gem after priceless whataboutism gem.

One of the more startling claims in Kriek's article is that South Africa was uninhabited before the Europeans settled there, building a "dynamic society"—echoing the early Zionists' claim that Palestine was "a land without a people for a people without a land":

Contrary to popular belief, the whites did not take the country from the blacks. When the Dutch settled in the Cape in 1652, they found a barren, largely unpopulated land. Together with French and German settlers, they built a dynamic society.

It was not until 100 years later, as they advanced across these vast unexplored territories that they met with the blacks who were moving south. Contrary to myth, the blacks were never run off their land. They settled in tribal lands of their own choice.[44]

Kriek then offers the South African version of Manifest Destiny, and colonialism as a "civilizing" presence, later paralleled in Israel's claim that it was the Israelis who "made the desert bloom," which suggests that the Palestinians did not have orchards of citrus and olive trees.

When the whites met the blacks, the blacks had no written language, no technological knowledge, no cure for infectious diseases. In the 20th century, economic activity organized by whites gradually drew blacks out of their tribal lands into the cash economy and into the cities.[45]

The Palestinians in Israel are better off than Arabs in any other part of the Arab world, including Palestinians living in other Arab countries, we are often told. Again, this is analogous to a claim made by supporters of apartheid South Africa. In Kriek's words again:

[South African] Blacks possess one of the highest living standards in all of Africa. Although black living conditions in South Africa (as in America) cover a wide spectrum, the housing is unequalled anywhere on the continent. Soweto is a proper city complete with schools, stores, theaters, sport stadiums and tennis courts. In some areas, blacks drive their children to private schools in German cars. Few states in black Africa can boast such a range of features. In Mamelodi (Pretoria) four-bedroom houses are made available to blacks at a total purchase price of $250.[46]

Mamelodi, by the way, is not in Pretoria itself, but just outside of the city, and was set up by the apartheid regime as a segregated, Blacks-only township. And these are the houses women would be expelled from, upon separation from the "man of the house." We then get treated to the direct attacks on neighboring countries, to best highlight South Africa's singularity as the only modern, civilized, "enlightened" country on that continent, just as today we are repeatedly told that Israel is "the only democracy in the Middle East." Thus, the article continues:

> Once vibrant, the 42 black-ruled states have now disintegrated into a political, social and economic nightmare. [...] Many of these states had one man one vote—but historically, only once. Those one-time elections were followed by one-party rule, or military dictatorships. In many countries it is practically impossible to vote the top leaders out of office. Any opposition always somehow just seems to disappear. The people are absorbed by the institutions of the ruling party.[47]

Ironically, Palestinians today do have a leader who is practically impossible to vote out of office, and that is Mahmoud Abbas. His term as president officially ended in 2009, yet he is still internationally recognized in that capacity. Finally, Kriek's article offers up more statistics about the misery of Tanzania, Kenya, Nigeria, Mozambique, Zimbabwe, before the concluding denunciation and questions:

> The western world closes its eyes to the true situation in Africa. All the hand wringing over South Africa turns to hand washing when it comes to condemning black Africa. The West soothes its conscience by injecting development aid. Nobody seems to have noticed that despite the aid, the situation keeps getting worse.

Why is South Africa so harshly condemned while completely different standards apply to black Africa? ...

Is it that one form of repression is more acceptable than another, or is it that black/white oppression hits home? Or is it maybe that better conduct is expected of a white-ruled country than from black-ruled Africa?[48]

As one explores the parallels between the arguments presented in 1989 in defense of apartheid South Africa, and those presented today in defense of apartheid Israel, one cannot help but wonder if today's Zionists are aware of how much they are recycling a discourse that was ultimately debunked.

The many similarities between South Africa and Israel notwithstanding, possibly the biggest difference between the struggle to end apartheid in South Africa, and today's struggle to end Israeli apartheid, is the fact that Palestinians do not have an equivalent of the African National Congress—a political party which also fully engaged in activism and resistance. This is not to suggest that the ANC was the only political party in South Africa, nor that it made no mistakes. Nevertheless, since its foundation in 1912, and despite significant setbacks that included bans, exiles, and imprisonment, the ANC pursued a cohesive course with an unwavering commitment to liberation, and a strategy to accomplish that goal. By contrast, the Palestinian political fragmentation today is such that there are two major political parties, Fatah and Hamas, neither of which has issued a strategic call for solidarity. Fatah, which initially was committed to national liberation through revolutionary struggle, has, over a series of egregious political mistakes initiated by Yasser Arafat, and continued by Mahmoud Abbas as president of the Palestinian Authority (PA), devolved into a dysfunctional and unpopular security apparatus for Israel's occupation of the West Bank. The PA's only "authority" is exercised to control Palestinians as they protest their oppression. The PA is also notorious for its misogyny, as denounced by Dr. Hanan Ashrawi in her resignation letter citing a lack of opportunity for women and young people. In 2019, the PA banned workshops around gender diversity that the Palestinian queer group alQaws had organized in the wake of the stabbing of a young Palestinian outside a Tel Aviv center for gay and transgender youths. More recently, plain-clothes PA security forces have targeted women journalists covering protests in Ramallah, threatening them with rape and defamation. Yet, Zionists have no qualms "negotiating" with the PA, because they know they can always secure more concessions from it. And they'll turn a blind eye to the PA's misogyny, because "WhatAboutHamas."

3

Social and Political Liberation: No Free Homeland Without Free Women and Queers

On the Indivisibility of Justice

Palestine is a feminist issue. The statement is a truism and should need no elaboration. Yet, as with so much that relates to Palestine, it has necessitated long discussions, clarifications, analysis, and ample documentation, again and again. Palestine rights activists have long been familiar with the sadly all too common phenomenon known as "PEP": Progressive Except for Palestine. Less known, but no less common in feminist circles is "FEP," Feminist Except for Palestine. Books like Evelyn Shakir's *Bint Arab* recount incidents of FEP going back to the 1960s, with numerous Arab feminists being shunned by their American friends over their support for Palestinian liberation.[1] FEP had one of its early expressions on a global stage at the 1985 United Nations World Conference on Women in Nairobi, Kenya, when Betty Friedan, an icon of second wave Western feminism, with its slogan "the personal is political," tried to censor the late Egyptian feminist Nawal El Saadawi as the latter was about to walk up to the stage to deliver her address. "Please do not bring up Palestine in your speech," Friedan told El Saadawi, "this is a women's conference, not a political conference."[2] Sadly, little has changed in Global North feminism's rejection of the very humanity of Palestinian women, as evidenced in their continued exclusion from national and global discussions of women's issues. Ten years after Friedan's patronizing remarks to El Saadawi, Hillary Clinton spoke at the 1995 World Conference on Women in Beijing, China, stating: "If there is one message that echoes forth from this conference, it is that human rights are women's rights ... And women's rights are human rights."[3] Clinton explained that:

> Our goals for this conference, to strengthen families and societies by empowering women to take greater control over their own destinies, cannot be fully achieved unless all governments—here and around the world—accept their responsibility to protect and promote internationally recognized human rights.[4]

Yet, Clinton never suggested that Israel should "accept its responsibility to protect and promote internationally recognized human rights." Years later, as Clinton continued to express admiration for Israel, Layali Awwad, then a student at Kenyon College, penned an Open Letter to the First Lady articulating what many other Palestinian feminists felt—our complete exclusion from "humanity" as defined by white feminism. Awwad points out to Clinton that:

> when you chose to speak about my homeland, not once did you mention Israel's human rights violations against Palestinian women and children. Even worse, you described us as lurking terrorists motivated only by "incitement," as if the Israeli military occupation does not exist.[5]

Awwad then documents the daily harassment and violence she and millions of Palestinian women and girls endure at the hands of Israeli soldiers, stating that, to Clinton, "we are invisible, like women have been treated throughout history."[6]

The saga of white feminism aligning itself with Orientalist imperialist militarism continued with *Ms. Magazine* cheering the Bush Administration's US war on Afghanistan, calling it a "coalition of hope," and suggesting that invasion and occupation could, indeed would, liberate Afghan women. The white feminists in the Feminist Majority Foundation, which bought *Ms. Magazine* in December 2001, never consulted with Afghan feminist organizations such as RAWA, the Revolutionary Association of the Women of Afghanistan, who denounced both religious fundamentalism and Western intervention in Afghanistan, and who opposed the US attacks on their country. Meanwhile, grassroots groups such as INCITE! Women of Color Against Violence were denouncing all militarism, and producing and widely distributing anti-war popular education resources including stickers, flyers, posters, and online analysis. One of their most popular posters reads "Invading armies have never liberated women of color and third world women! Only we can liberate ourselves."[7] INCITE! was among the earliest nationwide US feminist groups to fully support the struggle for Palestinian liberation, first by issuing their "Palestine Points of Unity," then by endorsing BDS (Boycott, Divestment, and Sanctions), shortly after the Palestinian call was issued. INCITE! also reprinted the groundbreaking essay, "The Forgotten '-ism': An Arab American Women's Perspective on Zionism, Racism, and Sexism," penned in 2001 by members of the Arab Women's Solidarity Association, in INCITE's anthology *The Color of Violence*.[8] That essay documents the long-standing anti-Arab racism in white feminist circles resulting from privileged white feminists' uncritical embrace of Zionism, which they view as liberatory, rather than oppressive.

More recently, hegemonic feminism's desire to exempt Israel from criticism led to the fragmentation of the Women's March, the coalition of women's and feminist groups that came together to denounce the election of Donald Trump to the presidency of the USA. The co-chair of the 2017 Women's March was Brooklyn-born Palestinian American Linda Sarsour, a grassroots organizer who had long championed Palestinian rights. Zionists felt threatened by Sarsour's outspokenness and visibility, with journalist Emily Shire publishing an OpEd in the *New York Times* asking: "Does Feminism have Room for Zionists?" to which Sarsour responded with a resounding: "No."[9]

Another Palestinian feminist, Mariam Barghouti, also published an article asserting that "No, You Can't Be a Feminist and a Zionist," and explaining that:

When I hear anyone championing Zionism while also identifying as a feminist, my mind turns to images of night raids, to the torture of children and to the bulldozing of homes. Being a feminist and a Zionist is a contradiction in terms because the Zionist feminist is complicit in propagating supremacy and domination over a people on the one hand, while on the other hand calling for an end to patriarchy.[10]

Quoting bell hooks' analysis of feminism as a complete liberatory movement, Barghouti then explains:

Feminism cannot be selective. Its framework comes from true and absolute liberation not just of women, but of all peoples. This is why Zionism and feminism cannot merge. A feminist who is not also anti-colonial, anti-racist and in opposition to the various forms of injustice is selectively and oppressively serving the interests of a single segment of the global community.[11]

Thankfully, today, progressive women of color and Indigenous women, along with anti-imperialist, anti-racist white women, are firmly anti-Zionist, understanding that no ideology that hinges on supremacy and discrimination is reconcilable with feminism. Simply, "feminism" that aligns with regimes that engage in racial and ethnic oppression is gendered supremacy.

The "Demographic Threat"

In Chapter 2, "Déjà Vu: Beyond Apartheid," I discussed some of the detrimental ways women suffer under legal discrimination, which continue to impact them long after that system is overthrown. And in Chapter 1, "Settler Colonialism and Indigenous Resistance from Palestine to Turtle Island," I felt it necessary to re-establish Zionism as a form of colonialism, because the recent focus on apartheid has obscured the root cause of Palestinian dispossession: not just legal disenfranchisement, but also land dispossession, and a dominant narrative that would erase the Palestinian people's long-standing presence in the country, turning them, rather than the settlers, into interlopers. I stated that colonialism is always gendered, an observation that numerous scholars have argued persuasively over the past few decades, as they analyzed the many ways women's bodies become the battlegrounds of power, either as proof of conquest, or as prime targets of the settler's desire to "eliminate the native." In addition to the violence of sexual assault, gendered violence takes on specific forms depending on the political, social, and cultural context of the colonial assault.

In her discussion of British colonialism in India, for example, Gayatri Chakravorty Spivak presents English men as would-be protectors, the white saviors "saving brown women from brown men."[12] Spivak criticizes the lack of an account of the Hindu cultural practice of sati in narratives that focus on the agency of Europeans saving "brown women," thus eclipsing any representations of the colonized. Yet, as the British colonizers banned the practice, they were demonizing the patriarchal culture, but viewed Indian women as its victims, redeemable, in need of the intervention of the white savior, who thus appears not as a colonizer, but as liberator.

In Algeria, French *colons* would round up Muslim Algerian women and publicly strip them of their headdress in a demonstration of how they were "modernizing" Algerian society. The veil, rather than imperialism, was viewed as oppressive—a trend that continues into modern-day Europe, where Muslim women are frequently barred from veiling in official and public spaces, in a gesture of cultural imposition that disrespects their piety, in order to "liberate" them from the directives of their faith. In colonial Algeria, this violence was not enacted by French men against Algerian women; rather, French women, especially the wives of French military officers, partook of this supposedly emancipatory assault, as they unveiled the Algerian women at these public spectacles of "sisterhood." Such imposition is a prime example of imperialist feminism, the white women's burden to intervene by any means necessary, including militarism and colonialism, to "emancipate" women deemed less fortunate, oppressed by their backward cultures. It is only appropriate to note that French women themselves had little autonomy under the French legal system at the time: they could not vote, and they needed their husband's approval to open a bank account or be employed outside the house. And the actual liberation of Algerian women was never the true goal, as they were to remain colonized—albeit without their veils. Similarly, in Egypt, Evelyn Baring, Earl of Cromer strongly denounced the veil as oppressive, even as he opposed women's suffrage in England. Palestinian American anthropologist Lila Abu-Lughod's 2002 article, "Do Muslim Women Really Need Saving?" as well as her 2015 book of the same name, are scathing indictments of colonial feminism and reveal the hypocrisy of seeking to "rescue" Muslim women while devastating their countries.[13]

The French colonizers are also infamous for their many photographic renderings of eroticized Muslim women drawing open their head-to-toe garments, to expose their naked bodies. These staged photographs were reproduced as postcards, which the colons would send home to the metropole, as if to claim their personal conquest. The postcards represented visual rape, when carnal violation was not always attainable. In The Colonial Harem, Algerian literary critic Malek Alloula argues that "orphans and prostitutes" were frequently forced to pose for these photos, which purported to somehow show women going about their everyday business—of sexual availability.[14] Of course the photographs were not spontaneous renditions of average Algerian women, rather, they represented a Frenchman's fantasy of the "Oriental female," fully exposed to the colonizer's voyeuristic gaze.

Palestinian women have fared no better under Israeli colonialism. Zionism, however, has never exoticized us, never purported to "save," "modernize," or "liberate" us. It has always wanted us dead. Even as violent Israelis, both men and women, today grab Palestinian women by their scarves, it is not to eroticize them for voyeuristic satisfaction, but strictly to assault, humiliate, and ultimately eliminate us. Zionism views Palestinian women as a demographic threat, the progenitors of future terrorists, "enemy combatants" raising "little snakes," as Knesset Member and far-right Yamina Party member Ayelet Shaked put it. In a post in Hebrew that was later translated into English, Shaked basically advocated genocide, as she wrote:

Behind every terrorist stand dozens of men and women, without whom he could not engage in terrorism ... They are all enemy combatants, and their blood shall be on all their heads. Now this also includes the mothers of the martyrs, who send them to hell with flowers and kisses. They should follow their sons, nothing would be more just. They should go, as should the physical homes in which they raised the snakes. Otherwise, more little snakes will be raised there.[15]

Shaked was serving as Israel's Justice Minister when she made that statement; she is Minister of the Interior at the time of this writing.

Other Zionists openly advocate the rape of Palestinian women as a weapon of war. Thus, a military advisor suggested that one way to coerce Hamas militants into ending their resistance is by raping their mothers and sisters. "The only thing that can deter terrorists, like those who kidnapped the children and killed them, is the knowledge that their sister or their mother will be raped," according to Mordechai Kedar, a lecturer at Bar-Ilan University, who added: "What can you do, it's the culture in which we live".[16]

Examples of Israel's violence against Palestinian women, from the months preceding the birth of the colonial country, into the present, are unfortunately plentiful. The rape and murder of Palestinian women was not a "side effect" of conquest, the proverbial "rape, pillage, loot" that accompanies military advances. Rather, it was a central aspect of the massacres leading to the establishment of the new state, as described in the diary entries of David Ben-Gurion, Israel's first prime minister.[17] Palestinian oral history recounts that, during the April 1948 Deir Yassin massacre, for example, a nine-month pregnant woman was killed before the Zionist militias cut her open and stole her unborn baby. When a Palestinian woman tried to take the baby away from the Zionist militiaman's grip, she was shot too. While this particular incident is hard to corroborate, its widespread oral circulation from 1948 to the present is proof of the gendered trauma experienced by Palestinians since the onset of al-Nakba: the Zionists kill us and steal our progeny, our future. Walid Khalidi's Arabic-language *Deir Yassin: Friday, 9 April, 1948*, remains one of the best books about the foundational massacre, with testimonies from thirty survivors, as well as accounts from some of the perpetrators of the crimes.[18] Testimonies collected after the massacre also recall that Palestinian women were raped in front of their children, before being shot and dumped by the roadside. All accounts of the massacre feature the wanton killing of unarmed women and children, the burning of the bodies of the killed to conceal details of the executions, and the parading of defeated survivors through nearby Jerusalem, as a warning to other Palestinians of the fate that would await them, should they resist attack.

Israeli historian Benny Morris also lists numerous acts of gang rape of Palestinian women by Zionist militiamen which he came across during his research into the 1948 fighting, noting that these are "just the tip of the iceberg":

In Acre four soldiers raped a girl and murdered her and her father. In Jaffa, soldiers of the Kiryati Brigade raped one girl and tried to rape several more. At Hunin, which is in the Galilee, two girls were raped and then murdered. There were one or two cases of rape at Tantura, south of Haifa. There was one case of rape at Qula, in the center of the country. At the village of Abu Shusha, near Kibbutz Gezer [in the Ramle area] there were four female prisoners, one of whom was raped a number of times. And there were other cases. Usually more than one soldier was involved. Usually there were one or two Palestinian girls. In a large proportion of the cases the event ended with murder. Because neither the victims nor the rapists liked to report these events, we have to assume that the dozen cases of rape that were reported, which I found, are not the whole story. They are just the tip of the iceberg.[19]

Following the rape and murder of Palestinian women at the onset of al-Nakba, Ben-Gurion in the 1950s turned his attention to the issue of Jewish women's fertility, shaming Israeli women who did not bear at least four children as having "failed their Jewish mission," and awarding those who bore ten children a special prize.[20] The Zionist paranoia about the Palestinian "demographic threat," the likelihood that Jews will

once again be a demographic minority in Palestine, has always politicized Palestinian women's reproductive issues, resulting in the many
restrictions on their access to health care while pregnant. Thus, Palestinian women in labor have routinely been detained and delayed at
checkpoints, and prevented from reaching a hospital. Many have given
birth at checkpoints, or by the side of the road, and newborn infants
have died for lack of neonatal care. A 2007 United Nations High Com-
missioner for Human Rights report detailing sixty-nine such incidents
remains unanswered by any Israeli officials.[21]

The need to deliver in a hospital, rather than at home, is itself an
Israeli population control strategy. As Rita Giacaman, Laura Wick,
Hanan Abdul-Rahim, and Livia Wick have documented, beginning in
1967, Israel stopped issuing licenses for "*dayat*," or traditional midwives,
to assist in home deliveries. But this was not out of concern for the
well-being of mother and newborn. Rather, "Promoting hospital births
meant that the Palestinian population could be more easily counted,
registered, identified and thus controlled. Knowledge and control are
potential tools in demographic strategy formulation, which are an
integral part of the Palestine–Israeli conflict."[22] Giacaman et al. argue
that promoting hospital births was not based on the health needs of the
population, nor was it reflected in an upgrade in existing services. They
write that:

> Whereas improvements in the infrastructure and the quality of care
> would have helped to stimulate the demand for births in the hospital,
> little was done to improve the conditions of the maternity units, con-
> firming the supposition that politics, control, and finances—rather
> than health needs and conditions—play an important role in public
> health decision-making, particularly in an occupied country.[23]

The hospitals were located in urban centers and, "for most Palestinians
therefore, transport to the hospital has become an integral and critical
part of the birthing process, which constantly preoccupies women, the
families, and their birth attendants."[24] Overall, it is estimated that 10
percent of pregnant women are detained and delayed at Israeli check-

points within the West Bank. In one study published in 2005, thirty-six
newborn infants had died at checkpoints from 2000 to 2005. Additionally, as Rhoda Kanaaneh documents in *Birthing the Nation*, whether
Palestinians believe that high fertility rates work in their favor in the
"demographic race" with Jews in Israel, or hold the position that "a few
highly educated, professional middle-class Palestinians are more challenging to Israeli domination than a lot of uneducated poor ones," advocates of both perspectives "have unwittingly accepted one of [Israel's]
basic premises by closely associating nationalism with reproduction
and women."[25]

Along with the politicization of motherhood, Israel has a long-standing and multifaceted practice of manipulating patriarchal and homophobic structures, especially conservative perceptions of "honor," to recruit
Palestinian collaborators and fragment Palestinian society. There are
reports of Israeli police taking photos of young women secretly meeting
a boyfriend, and threatening to report them to their parents unless
they divulge strategic information to Israel's intelligence services. One
former Israeli soldier says of such extortion:

I assumed a role in which people are called "targets," and those
people who really interest us are in no sense terrorists, but rather generally normative people—who interest us because of their roles, so
that we can obtain more intelligence and achieve greater access. We
take advantage of the capabilities that we have over these people in
order to put ourselves at ease. We take advantage of the impact that
we have on their lives. Sometimes it involves truly harming a person's
life, or their soul. I mean extortion whereby they must hide things
from people around them. It can really screw up their lives.[26]

The soldier adds that personal details like one's medical condition or
sexual orientation would also be used for intelligence gathering:

Any information that might enable extortion of an individual is considered relevant information. Whether said individual is of a certain

sexual orientation, cheating on his wife, or in need of treatment in Israel or the West Bank—he is a target for blackmail.[27]

There are also reported cases where women were unknowingly drugged, then photographed in compromising poses, and later told these photos would be made public if they do not divulge vital information about resistance efforts. Interrogators would also threaten to rape women unless they gave out information about resistance initiatives.

The threat is sometimes carried out, as in the documented case of Rasmea Odeh, who was arrested at the age of twenty-one in 1969, and tortured for twenty-five days, during which she was also raped in the presence of her father, during her interrogation.[28] Many detained Palestinian girls and women say they are searched and interrogated by male soldiers. More recently, in 2016, twelve-year-old Dima al-Wawi became the youngest female prisoner in Israeli jails. According to her mother, the twelve-year-old girl was:

treated in the most brutal way and underwent a terrifying and traumatic interrogation ... She was interrogated by at least seven officials who screamed, cursed and insulted her, and then threatened to burn her alive. She was stripped of her clothes and violently beaten.[29]

Dima told her mother she bled from the torture during interrogation and was made to "feel ashamed."[30] In her case too, no female soldier was present during interrogation. The slogan "al-ard qabl al-'ard," or "Land Before Honor," popularized after 1967, was meant to encourage Palestinian women not to be "shamed" into collaboration through such threats and blackmail. These tactics are especially devastating when the Mossad extorts closeted Palestinian queers, some of whom end up becoming collaborators for fear of being outed to their communities—a development that further stigmatizes queers and endangers their lives. Israel also makes ample use of the "honey trap," where Israeli Mossad members pose online as attractive European women, or men, to seduce Palestinian men, then blackmail them with the threat of scandal.

Intensifying Patriarchy

Colonized cultures, and cultures under attack, can understandably feel the need to preserve their traditional ways. This tendency sometimes comes from an impetus to "conserve" the pre-conquest culture, resulting in a suspension of changes which blocks what would otherwise have been a society's organic development. Additionally, as they are threatened with erasure, conquered cultures can uncritically hold on to a glorified, romanticized version of the past. In the case of Palestine, the more Israel proclaims itself to be a "liberal democracy," pro-women and pro-gay, and unique of its kind in the region, "the only democracy in the Middle East," the more reactionary elements within Palestinian society register gender and sexual justice as alien, colonial impositions. Feminism, women's rights, and particularly gay rights become associated with Israel, which indeed is weaponizing these concepts even as it is seeking the total annihilation of Palestinian culture. Coupled with the masculinist and militaristic environment Palestinians live in, the consequences of these associations are sometimes fatal. This regressive masculinism, or intensification of patriarchy and heteronormativity, has unfortunately manifested in many Palestinian communities, with a devastating effect on the lives and overall freedoms of Palestinian women and queers.[31] Today, gender-based violence within the family has reached alarming levels, with young women being murdered by their husbands, brothers, or fathers in a fatally misguided attempt to "save the family's honor." Indeed, even the slogan "Land Before Honor" does not uplift women, as much as it puts them in a subservient position to national liberation. Should they be sexually assaulted by Israelis as part of their participation in the anti-colonial struggle, Palestinian society might look away. But the conservative patriarchal Palestinian concept of "honor," that is, a woman's chastity, her virginity until her wedding day, and her overall submissiveness to patriarchal structures, while challenged, has not yet been overturned. Rather, it has become stricter as political and economic conditions have become more dire, because control over women serves as a form of cultural capital and, therefore, power. In an environment where men have diminishing opportunities to advance socially, it is in the domestic sphere that they exercise what little control society grants them.

This phenomenon—the intersectionality of the political, the social, and the economic—is not unique to Palestine, and has been analyzed by many women of color globally. The term "intersectionality" itself was first coined by Kimberlé Crenshaw in 1989 to describe how race, gender, class, and other individual characteristics intersect to create a compound structure of oppression that a single-axis framework (race and gender as parallel, rather than overlapping in the same person) cannot analyze adequately.[32] However, even as she is credited with coining the term, Crenshaw herself refers to earlier Black women who described the positionality of Black women at the nexus of various systems of oppression, with socio-economic class always being one of these. One year before Crenshaw's article, for example, Deborah King had published "Multiple Jeopardy, Multiple Consciousness: The Context of a Black Feminist Ideology," in which she argued that class inequality, a constant in the circumstances of Black Americans, compounds the systematic discriminations of racism and sexism.[33]

And in "Double Jeopardy: To Be Black and Female," Frances Beal had proposed that Black men, being denied pathways to heteropatriarchal "manhood" as defined by capitalist colonial criteria, re-exert violence and authority over those more vulnerable, in order to assert their "power."[34] "America has defined the roles to which each individual should subscribe," Beal wrote.

It has defined "manhood" in terms of its own interests and "femininity" likewise. Therefore, an individual who has a good job, makes a lot of money and drives a Cadillac is a real "man," and conversely, an individual who is lacking in these "qualities" is less of a man.[35]

Beal argued that because Black males have historically been denied opportunities to advance socially and economically, they exercise what they consider to be power over those individuals who are socially one rung below them: Black women. Like other Black feminists, Beal too refers to the activism and analysis of earlier Black women, particularly

Sojourner Truth, who in 1851 reportedly asked the question that resonates to this day: "Ain't I A Woman?"[36] Palestinian women have been asking this question of Zionists for decades, as we expose the hypocrisy of, say, Hillary Clinton, who asserted that "women's rights are human rights" even as she totally disregarded the egregious violations of Palestinian women's rights by Israel, a country she hails as a "light unto the nations."[37]

In 1976, the Black feminist Combahee River Collective had offered their own analysis of the multiple oppression of Black women, in their "Combahee River Collective Statement," where they name capitalism as one of the interlocking systems of oppression: "A combined anti-racist and anti-sexist position drew us together initially, and as we developed politically we addressed ourselves to heterosexism and economic oppression under capitalism."[38] The members of the collective were lesbians, and they also listed heterosexuality as one of the social privileges they do not have access to: "We do not have racial, sexual, heterosexual, or class privilege to rely upon, nor do we have even the minimal access to resources and power that groups who possess anyone of these types of privilege have."[39] Today, as they are situated at the intersection of race, gender, class, as well as the desire of Black men to "exercise their power," it is no accident that Black trans women are killed at disproportionately high rates compared to any other social group, and that their killers are most often their Black male intimate partners.[40]

A similar dynamic operates in Palestine, where Palestinian women's rights and lives are most endangered by Israel, but where Palestinian men exert additional violence, which they view as "power," over them, the more these men themselves are oppressed and denied access to the cultural indicators of manhood: political and spatial autonomy, and a job with an income that makes them the head of household. The "manhood" of Palestinian males is further threatened by the fact that they simply cannot protect their family members from Israel's military assaults, the bombings, arbitrary killings, detentions, and the daily humiliations of being a Palestinian living under Zionism. A man who cannot protect his family is somehow viewed as a greater failure than a woman who cannot do the same, because of the sexist assumption that women are essentially weaker, and dependent on men. In reality, there are endless examples of women being perfectly competent heads of their households, protecting and nurturing both their families and communities. "Those who are exerting their 'manhood' by telling black women to step back into a domestic, submissive role are assuming a counter-revolutionary position," Beal had written.[41] Similarly, it is counter-revolutionary to demand submission of Palestinian women, especially when one considers the important roles they have always played, and continue to play, in the struggle for liberation. But it gives Palestinian men the illusion of power they cannot otherwise have, under the crushing oppression of Zionism.

Also, in the USA, more than half of Indigenous women suffer physical violence at the hands of their intimate partners. Two in three Indigenous women experience rape at least once in their lifetime. And Indigenous women are murdered at rates as high as ten times those of all other ethnicities, with murder being the third leading cause of death for Indigenous women, after cancer and heart disease. However, unlike other women of color in the USA, who are mostly murdered by men of their own race, but like Palestinian women in historic Palestine, Indigenous women are disproportionately killed by non-Indigenous males—their colonizers.[42] Indigenous women have also argued that the violence they experience is directly related to colonialism. In *The Beginning and End of Rape*, Muscogee Creek feminist scholar Sarah Deer argues that violence against native women is political, a result of the gendered legacy of colonialism.[43] Indeed, the murder of Indigenous women today is most prevalent around "man camps," temporary housing units for transient workers in the oil extraction industry, which are frequently set up on reservation land itself.[44] As the Red Nation collective explains:

Because Indigenous bodies stand in the way of access to the land and because women are seen as the producers of native nations through the European heteropatriarchal lens, violence against women, particularly sexual violence, is used as means of separating native people from the land.[45]

Viewing Indigenous women as "producers of native nations" echoes the Zionist perception of Palestinian women "giving birth to little snakes." The Red Nation then explains the colonizers' attempt to control Indigenous women's reproductive rights: "After this era [of boarding schools for Indigenous children] Native women and families were stripped of their autonomy via forced sterilization, lack of access to prenatal and postnatal care, poor reproductive health services, poverty, assimilation, exotification, and objectification."[46] Again, let us recall that post 1967, when Israel occupied the West Bank and Gaza Strip, it stopped issuing licenses for traditional Palestinian *dayat* (midwives), and set up many obstacles to Palestinian women's access to reproductive health services. And while there may no longer be checkpoints within the Gaza Strip, the lack of access to health care there is unconscionable, as Israel has deprived the entire region of sanitation equipment, electricity, even sufficient food, and certainly freedom of movement. Consequently, a 2015 UN report shows that 25 percent of pregnant Palestinian women in the West Bank and Gaza risk death during childbirth, and 35 percent of children under five are at risk of not meeting their full developmental potential due to poverty, hunger, and lack of access to basic services.[47]

From Genocide to Femicide

Palestinian feminists have noted for many years how the intensification of patriarchal norms resulting from Zionist colonialism translates into horrific instances of femicide. Particularly, scholars Nadera Shalhoub-Kevorkian and Suhad Daher-Nashif have conducted numerous studies into femicide among Palestinian communities throughout historic Palestine. They argue that Zionist colonialism plays a significant role in increasing Palestinian women's vulnerability, as it creates an overarching structure of oppression that is compounded as it trickles down to the more vulnerable members of the colonized society.[48] The term "femicide" was first used by Shalhoub-Kevorkian in 2004 to refer to "all violent acts that instill a perpetual fear in women and girls of being killed under the justification of 'honor.'"[49] Shalhoub-Kevorkian, like many Arab feminists, refuses to refer to these murders as "honor crimes" because that term is used by the murderers themselves to legitimize the killings, when there is nothing "honorable" about these crimes. Additionally, Shalhoub-Kevorkian and Daher-Nashif argue that "the use of the term femicide instead of honor killings is considered critical to counter dominant culturalized depictions of such crimes."[50] They explain that in Orientalist discourse,

> the killing of women for the purpose of family "honor" is simply something intrinsic to "Arab culture," which is purportedly violent, misogynistic, barbaric, and backward. Although such culturalized explanations have *never* been sufficient or adequate when it comes to understanding femicide, they are especially important to challenge in this present period where imperial agendas deploy powerful images and icons of the oppression of Middle Eastern women as *casus belli* (italics in original).[51]

Shalhoub-Kevorkian and Daher-Nashif conclude their study of the interconnectedness of Israeli colonialism with the impoverishment and exclusion from power of Palestinian men thus:

> The study of crimes in colonized zones must never be divorced from the political contexts and workings of power that envelop them. The history of colonized societies and conflict zones are replete with examples of how hegemonic power-holders from both sides—the colonizer and the colonized—have used women's bodies and sexuality to empower themselves.[52]

In a more recent study focusing on femicide in the Gaza Strip, Daher-Nashif again points out that the number of women being murdered is rising alongside the increasing overall exclusion and poverty, thus stressing again that Palestinian women are exposed to multiple levels of abuse, including the political, social, and economic.[53]

It is in this context of intensifying patriarchy and rising rates of femicides that the Palestinian Youth Movement, a "transnational, independent, grassroots movement of young Palestinians in Palestine and in exile," issued its statement, "No Free Homeland Without Free Women." The immediate impetus for this statement was the murder of Israa' Ghrayeb, a twenty-one year old woman who had been beaten to death by three male relatives after posting a photo on Instagram with her fiancé, one day before the official engagement reception. Published on International Women's Day, March 8, 2020, the statement acknowledges the central role Palestinian women have played in the struggle to liberate their country, while affirming that "women's liberation is not secondary to national liberation."[54] They explain: "We recognize the entangled relationship between Zionist settler-colonial gendered violence and the intra-communal violence Palestinian women endure."[55] Quoting the Palestinian political prisoner Khalida Jarrar, the Palestine Youth Movement states:

Palestinians exist within a domain of colonial occupation, in which all Palestinians are denied freedom, and whereby women within the Palestinian society are doubly affected by structural and intra-communal and interpersonal violence. It is in this context that we recognize the impossibility of addressing communal and intimate violence against Palestinian women without contextualizing the broader racial, economic, and colonial structural oppressions that condition Palestinian society.[56]

The Palestinian Youth Movement (PYM), a predominantly diaspora group, was inspired by *Tal'at*, the Palestine-based collective who had taken to the streets by the thousands to protest rising violence against Palestinian women, and demand accountability for the femicides, and who had first popularized the slogan "No Free Homeland Without Free Women." *Tal'at* (Arabic for "stepping out," with a plural feminine declension) is a decentralized feminist collective that insists that true liberation must include the full emancipation of each and every Palestinian: men, women, gender non-conforming individuals, and children. They documented thirty-four cases of femicide in 2019 alone, while asserting that women's freedom is an intrinsic part of a homeland's freedom. Declaring "there is no honor in killing," *Tal'at* had taken to the streets chanting for refugee return, freedom, dignity, as well as an end to gender violence, and insisting that national aspirations can and should be reached through a feminist revolution. Like women of color in the USA, who named racialized capitalism as one of their oppressors, *Tal'at's* analysis also considers the impact of economic impoverishment on Palestinian society:

An actuality which cannot be sidelined from this matrix of oppression, is the systematic crippling of Palestinian economic development and the engineering [of] Palestinians, including women, into a cheap and exploitable workforce. This all culminates in a multilayered system of violence where power relations, in their gendered, economic, social and political forms, are intensified and reproduced, directly impact on intra-community social formations.[57]

And one year after the PYM International Women's Day statement, in March 2021, the Palestinian Feminist Collective (PFC), also diaspora based, was launched, asserting that "Palestine is a feminist issue" and explaining (yet again) that gendered and sexual violence is a weapon of war. "We commit to resisting gendered and sexual violence, settler colonialism, capitalist exploitation, land degradation and oppression in Palestine, on Turtle Island, and globally," and "We uphold the legacies of solidarity between Palestinian, Black, Indigenous, Third World feminist, working class, and queer communities who have struggled side-by-side within larger anti-colonial, anti-capitalist, and anti-racist movements in the US and globally."[58] All three groups, *Tal'at*, PYM, and the PFC, understand the complexity of seeking full liberation within a political context where the Palestinian Authority (PA), the official representative of the Palestinian people, is itself an extremely patriarchal political apparatus that upholds Israel's colonial violence and duplicates its methods of surveillance, threats, and blackmail. In the summer of 2021, for example, when Palestinians were protesting the PA's assassination of Palestinian dissident Nizar Banat, PA thugs arrested women, stole their cell phones, and threatened to publish private information and photos if they did not comply with security demands.[59] Yet, this understanding also allows for a transformational feminist visioning of liberation outside the confines of the nation state, and in solidarity with other colonized communities.

No Pink Door in the Apartheid Wall

As already noted, the threat of publishing potentially incriminating personal details is a standard Israeli intelligence-gathering tactic. Particularly, Israel jeopardizes gay Palestinians' lives by threatening to out them to conservative parents, a practice that has become known as "*isqat siyasi*."[60] Some do end up collaborating with Israeli agencies—as do straight Palestinians, of course—thus adding to the stigma of queers as socially deviant. Israel's exploitation of the challenging circumstances of queer Palestinians who do not have the support of family and community is particularly egregious considering its claim to be a "gay haven," and "the only gay friendly country in the region." This friendliness, however, does not extend to queer Palestinians, who engage with the complexity of their circumstances as at once colonized and gender non-conforming. As alQaws for Sexual and Gender Diversity in Palestinian Society put it in their analysis of Israel's colonial violence, "there is no pink door in the apartheid wall."[61]

AlQaws (Arabic for "the rainbow") which formed in 2001, is one of a handful of Palestinian organizations advocating for LGBTQ+ rights in Palestine, and along with other such groups, has long denounced pinkwashing, Israel's campaign to present itself as gay friendly. The pinkwashing campaign is part of an official propaganda campaign, "Brand Israel," itself the brainchild of US-based public relations experts concerned with fixing Israel's image. In 2005, three of Israel's most powerful ministries, namely, the Prime Minister's Office, the Foreign Ministry, and the Finance Ministry, concluded years of consultation with American media experts concerned with Israel's image, and the "Brand Israel" campaign was officially adopted. It aimed at appealing to two target American markets: "liberals," and youth between the ages of 16–30. Conservatives were staunchly pro-Israel, so there was little need to make a focused effort to retain them within the Zionist camp.

But support for Israel was waning primarily among liberals, which is why the rebranding campaign sought to appeal to liberal causes and priorities, rather than conservative ones, hence indigeneity ("redwashing"), environmentalism ("greenwashing," which we will discuss in Chapter 4) and gay rights, or "pinkwashing."[62] And a small country half a world away where there was a "conflict" that was "very complicated" and "had been going on for centuries" held little interest for most young Americans. Thus Israel21c, one of the companies involved in Brand Israel, states on its website that it "steer[s] clear from the narrow frame of conflict" to bring a "clear, unbiased reflection of life in Israel."[63] Israel21c, founded in 2001 and based in San Francisco, is closely associated with AIPAC, the staunchly Zionist American Israel Public Affairs Committee.

"Brand Israel" aims to distract from Israel's horrific record of human rights abuses and violations of international law by shining a bright light on the country's cultural accomplishments and its cosmopolitan culture. And since the pesky topic of war could not quite be avoided, in 2007, the Israeli Consulate General arranged a photo shoot titled "Women of the Israeli Defense Forces" in a special issue of *Maxim* magazine. An accompanying article reads: "They're drop-dead gorgeous and can take apart an Uzi in seconds. Are the women of the Israeli Defense Forces the world's sexiest soldiers?"[64] However, in 2009, shortly after "Operation Cast Lead," which killed over 1,400 Palestinians, most of them civilians, and wounded over 5,000 in the Gaza Strip, Arye Mekel, the Israeli Foreign Ministry's deputy director general for cultural affairs, shied away from glorifying the military, explaining instead: "We will send well-known novelists and writers overseas, theatre companies, exhibits. This way you show Israel's prettier face, so we are not thought of purely in the context of war."[65] Today, pinkwashing is one aspect of Israel's official propaganda campaign, and presents Israel as an oasis of gay freedom in an otherwise violently homophobic backwards region. Many of Israel's cultural ambassadors are gay men and women, promoting Israel's "liberal" record on gay rights.

Also in 2009, in the wake of Israel's murderous assault on Gaza, the International Gay and Lesbian Travel Association chose to highlight

Tel Aviv, with the American Israel advocacy organization StandWithUs telling the *Jerusalem Post*: "We decided to improve Israel's image through the gay community in Israel; we found that the issue is not familiar around the world."[66] Pitting "liberal Israel" against "homophobic Palestine," Noa Meir, who had a fellowship with StandWithUs, added: "We know that gays around the world are liberal usually and they tend to identify with the Palestinians, and we find it a bit ironic because you can't really be gay in the Palestinian territories."[67]

Pinkwashing, then, is the twenty-first-century manifestation of the imperial European narrative of bringing "civilization" to countries colonized by Europe. As Jasbir Puar put it:

Israeli pinkwashing is a potent method through which the terms of Israeli occupation of Palestine are reiterated—Israel is civilised, Palestinians are barbaric, homophobic, uncivilized, suicide-bombing fanatics. It produces Israel as the only gay-friendly country in an otherwise hostile region. This has manifold effects: it denies Israel's homophobic oppression of its own gays and lesbians, of which there is plenty, and it recruits, often unwittingly, gays and lesbians of other countries into a collusion with Israeli violence towards Palestine.

In reproducing orientalist tropes of Palestinian sexual backwardness, it also denies the impact of colonial occupation on the degradation and containment of Palestinian cultural norms and values. Pinkwashing harnesses global gays as a new source of affiliation, recruiting liberal gays into a dirty bargaining of their own safety against the continued oppression of Palestinians, now perforce rebranded as "gay unfriendly". The strategy then also works to elide the presence of numerous Palestinian gay and lesbian organisations, for example Palestinian Queers for Boycott, Divestment, and Sanctions.[68]

Puar had traveled to Palestine in 2011 with a delegation of sixteen US-based LGBTQ+ academics and activists organized by alQaws, Aswat (Arabic for "Voices," a Palestinian lesbian organization), and Jewish American queer writer and activist Sarah Schulman. AlQaws for Sexual and Gender Diversity in Palestinian Society, which first formed in Jerusalem, has since grown into a national organization with four hubs across historic Palestine. It has always understood and argued that the struggle takes place simultaneously on multiple fronts, whereas Israel seeks to project the struggle of queer Palestinians as a single-issue struggle to achieve "gay rights," that is, visibility, coming out, and pride events, with no mention of all the freedoms that queer Palestinians aspire to. In a May 2021 article, alQaws wrote:

> Queer liberation is fundamentally tied to the dreams of Palestinian liberation: self-determination, dignity, and the end of all systems of oppression. In a settler colonial context, no clear line can be drawn where colonialism ends and patriarchal violence begins. The fight against patriarchy and sexual oppression is intertwined with the fight against settler-colonialism and capitalism.[69]

Articulating a core tenet of intersectional liberatory politics, alQaws also denounces pinkwashing, as it writes:

> Israeli settler colonialism, and tactics such as "pinkwashing" weaponize our queer experiences to place us in opposition to our own society and communities. Pinkwashing is a form of colonial violence. It promotes harmful narratives and policies that alienate queer Palestinians from our own communities. Our answer to pinkwashing is to say that liberation is indivisible, and that there will be a place for all of us at the rendezvous of victory.[70]

Aswat, the Palestinian Feminist Center for Gender and Sexual Freedoms, has also denounced pinkwashing as a propaganda campaign, a cynical use of gay rights "to obfuscate the reality of occupation and apartheid," as Ghadir Shafie, co-founder and director of the organization, argues below.[71]

"Disappearing" the Palestinians

The outward aspect of pinkwashing—global propaganda to refurbish Israel's liberal image while deflecting from its ongoing crimes—while still worthy of denunciation, has thankfully been amply documented.[72] However, it is also important to analyze the specific ways pinkwashing works internally, within historic Palestine, to fragment Palestinian society, erase the cultural identity of Palestinian queers, and contribute to the erasure of all of Palestinian history thus further hurting queer Palestinians. First, by contrasting "gay friendly Israel" with "gay unfriendly Palestine," pinkwashing not only glosses over the extreme homophobia in Israeli society outside of the Tel Aviv bubble, but it also elides the presence of numerous Palestinian and Palestinian Diaspora queer organizations, such as alQaws, Aswat, or PQBDS (Palestinian Queers for Boycott, Divestment and Sanctions), as well as the many valuable contributions of queer Palestinians to the decolonial struggle. Additionally, as settler colonialism seeks "the elimination of the native," and pinkwashing is a weapon of settler colonialism, pinkwashing in reality contributes to the elimination of all Palestinians, including queers. Shafie, the co-founder of Aswat, recounts that, as a teenager questioning her sexuality, she was told (by an Israeli-staffed hotline) to move to Tel Aviv, where she would be able to live freely, "as a lesbian."[73] She applied to and got into Tel Aviv University.

The move to Tel Aviv was overwhelming. There, I thought, I would explore my sexuality and live freely, without having to hide, to be closeted, to cease to exist in so many ways. I was introduced to early 90s gay life in Tel Aviv through its vibrant bars and late-night gay parties, and made many gay Israeli friends. It didn't take long to realize that they were friendly to me as a lesbian while constantly trying to conceal, even suppress, my Palestinian identity. They affirmed that I did not look and sound Arab—so there was no need for me to embarrass them by bringing up my Palestinian-ness in conversations with others. I protested that my name clearly showed I was Arab. That was when they proposed changing my name for me.[74]

At the end of her first year at Tel Aviv University, Shafie left, "determined never to look back."[75] Shafie discusses pinkwashing as an "internal political strategy to contain radical Palestinian dissent and keep Palestinians at a constant disadvantage. "Excluding Palestinians from the 'gay haven' Tel Aviv—an experience many of us have been through—is merely symptomatic," Shafie writes, adding that:

Israel's pinkwashing policies run much deeper, functioning on a systemic level to alienate the "gay" Palestinian from their community, neutralize their potentially radical politics in favor of a bourgeois and domesticated "gay" identity, and thereby limit possibilities for radical change and mobilization in Palestinian societies.[76]

Thus, whereas neither Israeli nor Palestinian society are particularly gay friendly, by presenting itself as such, and distinguishing itself from Palestinian society precisely on that basis, Israel catalyzes Palestinian homophobia, now shrouded as "cultural." And as "gay friendly" becomes associated with the oppressor, it is now viewed with the same suspicion as "feminism," as a Western imperial imposition that must be resisted. Pinkwashing, then, as it attempts to refurbish Israel's image by projecting it as gay friendly, actively harms Palestinian gays, seeking to extricate them from their homeland, both physically and symbolically.

This "disappearing" of queer Palestinians is evident in the 2012 Israeli documentary *The Invisible Men*, which follows Louie, a gay Palestinian, as he flees his conservative family in the West Bank and moves to Tel Aviv.[77] Because he is Palestinian from the West Bank, Louie, and other gay Palestinians who have taken temporary refuge in Tel Aviv, are "illegal," and cannot live in Israel.[78] Instead, pro-bono Israeli lawyers arrange for their departure from the country. As Abdou, another gay Palestinian Louie meets in Tel Aviv, puts it: "The Palestinians won't accept us because we are gay, and the Israelis won't accept us because we are Palestinians without permits." Eventually, both Louie and Abdou are granted asylum in an unnamed European country, because Israel will not let them stay. *The Invisible Men* has been accused of pinkwashing because it received Israeli government funding, and was sponsored, in the USA, by "A Wider Bridge," a LGBTQ+ specific Israel advocacy organization that denies pinkwashing even exists. Yariv Mozer, the director and narrator of the documentary, explains that granting gay Palestinians asylum in Israel would be a "thorny issue," as it would be setting a precedent for the Right of Return.[79] Obviously, even when, or maybe especially because, their presence there is viewed as the practice of the inalienable human Right of Return, Palestinian gays are not allowed to exist in Tel Aviv, as we saw with Ghadir Shafie's experience. And for Louie, departure is not his first choice: "I want to breathe my culture, my land. I really don't want to go abroad," he says.[80] But Israel's "gay friendliness" does not extend to him.

Another film, Michael Lucas' 2009 Men of Israel, takes the erasure of all Palestinians to extremes of denial not encountered since Golda Meir's infamous argument that the Palestinians "did not exist." Men of Israel is a gay pornographic movie filmed in part in the cordoned off ruins of Lifta, which Lucas describes as an "abandoned village just north of Jerusalem. It was a beautiful ancient township that had been deserted centuries ago."[81] Yet contrary to Lucas' claim, Lifta has not been "deserted" for "centuries," but was ethnically cleansed in April 1948, one of over five hundred towns and villages forcibly depopulated in 1947–1949. Lifta is unique, however, in that its Palestinian residents have succeeded in having it designated as a World Heritage Site, thus preventing its destruction. As such, it is today, in the terms of the settler state, "the only abandoned Arab village in Israel not to have been destroyed or repopulated since 1948."[82] For Lucas, however, "that did not stop our guys from mounting each other and trying to repopulate it. Biology may not be the lesson of the day, but these men shot their seeds all over the village." There is certainly no need for Lucas' actors to "challenge biology" in their attempt to repopulate Lifta. Many of its original, Palestinian inhabitants and their children, and grandchildren, are still alive, some living only minutes away from the cordoned village, and they want nothing more than to return to their homes.

Unlike Mozer, who tried to dissociate his documentary from Israel's propaganda campaign, Lucas is very open about his promotion of "gay Israel" as refurbishing Israel's image. A Russian-Israeli-American gay porn mogul who once owned a travel agency, Lucas writes, on the official website of Men of Israel, that:

the global media has created an image of Israel as a war-torn nation, whose streets are lined with destroyed debris and crumbling ruins. Publicly broadcasted footage is always filmed in either Gaza or the West Bank, regardless of whether or not the story has a pro or anti-Israeli angle. Never are we shown Tel Aviv, Haifa, the Red Sea, the Dead Sea resorts, the beautiful beaches, the amazing architecture and the embracing culture that allows its citizens to thrive. For this reason, other than showcasing the raw, sexual prowess of Israeli men, Lucas also has completed MEN OF ISRAEL as a bold move to promote Israeli culture and tourism.[83]

Lucas, whose primary residence is in New York City, has also been politically involved in the gay activist scene there, mainly by blocking events critical of Israel, and specifically of pinkwashing. In early 2011, he protested a fundraiser by the group Siege Busters, which called for lifting the siege on Gaza, that was scheduled to be held at the New York LGBT Center, and later that year, he also succeeded in pressuring the center into cancelling a meeting of QuAIA (Queers Against Israeli Apartheid), accusing the two groups of antisemitism, and threatening to organize a campaign to end funding for the center, which caved in and decided to no longer host any events related to Israel and Palestine.

These examples, and there are many more, show that pinkwashing is not concerned with the plight of queer Palestinians, as much as it is with redeeming Israel in the eyes of liberals outside the country. Wielding women's and gay rights in a colonial context is a weaponizing of these rights that harms, rather than helps, the targeted communities. The recent resurgence of homophobic attacks on queer individuals and organizations in Palestine can be attributed in no small part to pinkwashing which, by positing the strict binary between "gay friendly Israel" and Palestine, suggests that achieving queer rights is an exclusively Western, Zionist aspiration, which detracts from the anticolonial struggle.

4

On This Land: Land and Cultural Reclamation from Turtle Island to Palestine

As we saw earlier, the most distinguishing characteristic of settler colonialism is that it is land theft. Consequently, decolonization in a settler colonial context must include land restitution. The first part of this chapter discusses the intentional environmental and cultural devastation wreaked by European colonizers as they seek to mold the stolen lands into their image. It also looks at how liberal conservationists and environmentalists continue to appropriate Indigenous lands for settler leisure in the Americas. This trend is epitomized in Woodie Guthrie's song "This Land is Your Land," and in the Sierra Club's "Hands Off Our Land" campaign, which promotes the defense of "public lands," thus shifting ownership and stewardship of Turtle Island to settlers. It should be noted that the US government owns 28 percent of the land of this country, with national parks alone accounting for 85 million acres, all stolen from Indigenous nations. Land restitution, beginning with stewardship of these parks, would be a good first step toward reparations. It would also alleviate the current climate crisis, as the Indigenous nations have historically managed the land more sustainably than the settler government or individual settlers. Anishinaabeg environmental activist and economist Winona LaDuke correctly points out that "There are millions of acres of national parks and monuments that should be, like Alcatraz, returned to Native people," a reminder that various treaties stipulate the return of federal land to Indigenous nations.[1]

Meanwhile, in Israel, "greenwashing" has long been a standard feature of Israeli propaganda, from the early assertion that Zionists "made the desert bloom," to the claim that Israeli conservationist societies are concerned about the extinction of certain native plants, to boasting about the Israeli military being environmentally friendly because it caters to its vegan soldiers. What Palestinians experience, however, is the poisoning and desertification of their lands, the theft of their water, the criminalization of their foraging traditions, and the uprooting of thousands of their ancient olive trees. As for the vegan Israeli soldiers, they drop bombs, not falafel patties, on Palestinian homes, schools, and hospitals.

In the second part, by focusing on food—a community's essential sustenance—we examine some of the many initiatives by the colonized to reclaim Indigenous lands, revive Indigenous cultures, and revitalize Indigenous ways. In so doing the Indigenous peoples are not only improving their devastated communities' quality of life, but also, simply, keeping the earth alive. The urgent necessity of land restitution is best put by the Red Nation Collective, when they insist that the choice before us is stark: "decolonization or extinction." This simple statement articulates the understanding that colonialism itself must be dismantled, if life on earth is to be preserved. Dismantling colonialism entails reversing its harmful effects on both the environment and the Indigenous nations it dispossessed and displaced. The land acknowledgments that are now routine among liberals in the USA and Canada are worthless when they are not accompanied by land restitution. They may lessen settler guilt, they do not, in themselves, redress any wrongs. "Land Back" is not a symbolic statement, it is an abolitionist call to action in the specific form of returning the land, and stewardship of the land, to the Indigenous people.

To put this in context, police abolitionists argue—correctly—that "reforming" the police only allows for a continuation of a force that is and always has been, from its very inception, essentially violent and racist. The motto of most police forces in the USA, namely, "to serve and protect," fails to mention that the police serve and protect property owners, not the needy and racialized. In the US South, many of today's police forces started out as slave patrols, seeking to capture runaway enslaved Africans escaping to freedom. They were serving white slaveowners, protecting these owners' control over their human "property." In the North, police forces started out as anti-labor squads, squashing protests for better work conditions. Those protests were mostly led by racialized communities: the Irish and Italian, deemed "un-American" because they were predominantly Catholic. Indeed, the racism of the Boston police force, for example, was evident early on with the controversy over the appointment of its first Irish officer, Bernard McGinniskin in late 1851. The anti-Irish sentiment was such that McGinniskin was fired within two months. After some criticism from the press, he was reinstated, only to be discharged again in 1854, simply on the grounds of his being Catholic. Repression of, and violence against the disenfranchised, racialized, and marginalized—frequently because of gender—is not a sad development in policing, rather it has always been the mission of police forces. Nor is "law enforcement" necessarily moral: some of the greatest crimes against humanity, from slavery to apartheid to colonialism, were "legal." Meanwhile, moral acts such as involvement in the Underground Railroad, or sheltering Jews during the Holocaust, were illegal. Hence, "reforming" the police can only be cosmetic; it will not transform the departments into support systems for the oppressed, abused, and communities of color. Indeed, abolitionists do not speak of "police brutality"; they understand that policing *is* brutality.

Similarly, Land Back activists argue—also correctly—that transferring ownership of stolen land from the government to "the American public" is not decolonization. The Sierra Club, as we will see, is not the Timbisha Shoshone nation; it is at odds with the ways and values of Indigenous nations. There is no such thing as kinder, gentler colonialism; colonialism *is* violence. On the other hand, careful tending of the land with an eye to collective healing, sustainability, and community empowerment, rather than corporate profit and individual enrichment, is an Indigenous feminist value, as articulated by La Via Campesina, who first popularized the expression "food sovereignty." Feminists of color's understanding of feminism is not one of wanting a bigger piece of the pie, but rather, one of wanting a different pie altogether, made with healthier, nourishing, sustainable ingredients.

"As American as Apple Pie"

The expression "as American as apple pie" is an adequate representation of the transformation of Turtle Island, from Indigenous to European. Apples are not native to the Americas, and apple pie is a European concoction, more calorific than nutritious. The transformation did not happen naturally, organically. Rather, despite their stated desire to start afresh, in "the new world," most settlers sought to shape their American environment according to what they were familiar with in "the old world." Additionally, settler colonialism is a zero-sum game: the settlers must destroy, so as to replace. If the Europeans were to claim dominion over Turtle Island, they had to eliminate the native peoples, as well as eradicate the native ways. This was best accomplished by destroying the native environment.

The USA is founded upon the genocide of the Indigenous nations. Massive as it is, the magnitude of this unnatural disaster is frequently overlooked, especially when compared to other genocides throughout history: the Tutsis, Armenians, Darfuri, the Holocaust, and so many more, which are generally commemorated with a day of sorrow, not gratitude (as with the US holiday of Thanksgiving). Even when it is not denied outright, the genocide of nations Indigenous to Turtle Island is somewhat explained away through arguments that not all the Indigenous were intentionally killed; some unfortunately succumbed instead to germs they had never encountered before, and which they had no immunity to: smallpox, measles, the flu. These diseases, however, would not have been as devastating were it not for the considerable influx of Europeans, and the overall weakening of the Indigenous populations due to the many wars they had to fight. Today, it is estimated that from 1492 to 1600, 90 percent of the Indigenous people in North America—approximately 60 million, or 10 percent of the entire population of the earth at the time—succumbed to wars and disease.[2] Yet, even after the quasi-elimination of most of the Indigenous peoples, the European colonizers were not satisfied, and forced the survivors off their traditional lands, onto reservations. The Indian Removal Act of 1831 gave US President Andrew Jackson the power to make treaties with every nation east of the Mississippi, ultimately resulting in their land dispossession and removal to "Indian Territory" in Oklahoma. Millions died during the trek, and civilian settlers joined the US Army in fighting those nations that refused to relocate.

One way they did so was by starving them into submission. Major General Philip Sheridan, who was charged with forcing the Indigenous nations off the plains, had learned, through his service in the army under Major General William Tecumseh Sherman, that one way to defeat the enemy was by destroying their resources: Sheridan is credited with the first uses of "scorched earth" tactics in the wars against the Confederate forces during the American Civil War. He implemented that same strategy in his wars against the Plains Indians. He determined to exterminate the buffalo, which sustained them. In October 1868, Sheridan wrote to Sherman that their best hope to control the Indigenous was to "make them poor by the destruction of their stock, and then settle them on the lands allotted to them." The strategy soon became routine: ecofeminist Carolyn Merchant recounts in her book, *American Environmental History*, that an army commander told the hunters of these massive beasts to "Kill every buffalo! Every buffalo dead is an Indian gone."[3] Within years, close to 40 million of this majestic animal were slaughtered.

Along with the forced removal of Indigenous nations to distant reservations that could not sustain them, the Europeans sought to literally form the continent's landscape into their own image. Mount Rushmore, for example, which was carved into the Black Mountains, transformed sacred Indigenous land into a monument to colonialism. The sculptor in chief, Gutzon Borglum, was a Ku Klux Klan sympathizer. One of the American presidents portrayed there is Theodore Roosevelt, who infamously said: "I don't go so far as to think that the only good Indians are the dead Indians, but I believe nine out of every 10 are."[4] Mount Rushmore is but one of the many examples of the violent transformation of the entire landscape of Turtle Island: monuments to the settlers, carved by settlers, desecrate the lands from which the Indigenous were forcefully displaced. This desecration is ongoing, with Euro-Americans today running pipelines through sacred land in the Standing Rock

Sioux Reservation, or installing a thirty-meter telescope on Mauna Kea, the most sacred mountain in Hawaii.

Meanwhile, as a result of losing access to their traditional food sources, the tribes became increasingly dependent on European staples in their diet, leading to significant health complications. Many nations who relied on mesquite beans, for example, could no longer access these when they were living on reservations. Mesquite beans are naturally full of protein and fiber and were traditionally ground into a gluten-free flour to make a tortilla or flatbread. Similarly, pine nuts are a protein-rich source, which many relocated nations could no longer access. Even when some federally recognized tribes secured their right to fish, hunt, or harvest according to their traditional ways, they were harshly criticized in the 1960s and 1970s by "progressive environmentalists" who argued that they were harming the environment. To this day, many Indigenous people report harassment when practicing their fishing rights off-reservation. Among the many examples of such harassment are the Indigenous fishermen in Minnesota having their car tires slashed while they are catching fish, hearing multiple gunshots in their direction while fishing, having strobe flashlights pointed at tribal spearfishermen, and rocks thrown at tribal members.[5] In Michigan, the Anishinaabeg, who include the Ojibwe, Odawa, and Potawatomi, ceded tens of millions of acres to the US government in the 1800s, but kept rights to hunt, fish, and gather on that land. The government of Michigan, however, totally ignored these rights, and arrested and fined the Indigenous hunters, fisher people, and gatherers. It is impossible not to see the similarities between the US government's treatment of the Indigenous nations here, and Israel's preventing fishermen in the Gaza Strip from catching fish in their own territorial waters. Only when the Indigenous nations fought back and won their cases in court again, affirming rights that were legally theirs, did the government stop ticketing them. But angry non-Natives have not stopped harassing and threatening them, vandalizing their fishing nets and boats, and occasionally firing weapons in their direction.[6] In the Southwest, environmental activists also opposed the hard-fought campaign by the Timbisha Shoshone people to engage in traditional land maintenance in 2000.

When the Shoshone and their allies finally secured the right to manage parts of Death Valley National Park, and sought to maintain it in the traditional ways, which include ritual fires, white environmentalists opposed that. Yet those fires were part of the Shoshone's traditional stewardship of the land, helping ensure food, medicinal, and ceremonial plants. By clearing streams cluttered with brush, the fires also increased water flow to the otherwise arid region.[7]

The tensions between white-led environmental groups and Indigenous nations are indicative of the irreconcilability of settler colonialism with Indigenous self-determination and sovereignty. This is best illustrated by the immense popularity of Woody Guthrie's folk song "This Land is Your Land," which reaffirms the settler belief in Manifest Destiny, as it repeats the chorus: "From the Redwood Forest to the Gulf Stream water/This land was made for you and me." Guthrie's song was meant to be critical of private property, but by asserting "public" (settler) ownership of the land by Guthrie and his listeners, it basically reinforces colonial entitlement and denies the Indigenous rights to their homelands. Similarly, the Sierra Club, one of the largest environmental preservation organizations in the USA, also uncritically asserts that the national parks are "public property" for all Americans—again claiming ownership of land violently acquired from its Indigenous stewards. The Sierra Club was founded by John Muir, still frequently referred to as "the father of the environmentalist movement." Yet Muir was a deeply racist colonizer who believed this continent was better protected by the settlers than by its own native stewards.[8]

Dispossessed, disconnected from their ancestral land, impoverished, unsettled, many developed diseases once unknown or extremely uncommon in their communities: obesity, diabetes, hypertension. And sexual violence, one of the longest lasting tools of conquest and dispossession, further aggravated these ravages, as it inflicted, and continues to inflict, multigenerational damage to the impacted communities. Today, the crisis of missing and murdered Indigenous women, girls, and two-spirit people (MMIWG2S) is making national news. But as many activists point out, what is frequently missing from the discussion of this femicide are the abusive conditions these women and gender non-conforming individuals lived in, before they were murdered. Sarah Deer, and the Red Nation collective, address the rampant sexual and domestic violence within Native households, both on and off reservations, that make the Indigenous vulnerable to greater violence from outsiders and the state. Particularly in *The Beginning and End of Rape*, Deer expounds on how rape was used by the federal government to create the destructive cultural implosion within Indigenous communities. "Rape is more than a metaphor for colonization," Deer writes, "it is integral to colonization."[9] Deer's book documents the rape of Native women by Spanish and Mexican soldiers, settlers, and ultimately, by Native men too, after these men were driven to internalize views about the lower social status accorded to women in Western culture. Today, the presence of "man camps" around pipeline projects running through Indigenous land increases sexual violence against Indigenous women. Widespread rape also disrupted the economic and social roles of women in Indigenous societies, Deer writes, giving the example of the Paiute nation, where women were once the primary food gatherers, but had to stop that practice because of the significant dangers from exposure to the predatory acts of the settlers.[10] As colonialism impacted women's social status and economic independence, especially by preventing them from engaging in their traditional farming, seed saving and exchange, and cooking ways, women also became more vulnerable to gender violence both within and outside of their communities.

This is why La Via Campesina (LVC), an international peasants' movement for food sovereignty, has always centered women's struggle in their analysis. One of its partner organizations in Palestine is the Union of Agricultural Work Committees (UAWC), one of the six human rights organizations designated as "terrorist" by Israel in October 2021. The UAWC provides hands-on help to tens of thousands of Palestinian farmers in the West Bank. The list sparked international outrage and was roundly denounced by human rights defenders, and foreign governments who read the seventy-four-page dossier prepared by Israel to support its accusations, refused to cut ties with these organizations, as the report failed to substantiate its own claims. Another Palestinian human rights organization on Israel's 2021 "terrorist list" is the Union of Palestinian Women's Committees—a clear indication of Israel's war on Palestinian land and women. In a statement issued shortly after the list was published, the Palestinian Feminist Collective noted:

By addressing diverse issues like the protection of children's rights, the defense and exoneration of political prisoners, the preservation and cultivation of indigenous agricultural practices, and the material improvement of women's lives, the work of all of the [targeted] organizations has long sustained and affirmed Palestinian life and land in the face of masculinist militarism, settler-colonial violence, racialized imprisonment and dispossession. Because of their critical work to advance safety, justice, and freedom, standing with the targeted organizations is an urgent feminist matter.[11]

Making the Desert Burn

In 1895, within mere decades of President Jackson's signing of the Indian Removal Act, followed by Sheridan's plans to starve and relocate the Indigenous nations, Austrian Theodor Herzl proposed that the only way to get rid of the Palestinians is to deceive those who are wealthy property owners, and impoverish the rest to the point that they would leave. "We shall try to spirit the penniless population across the border by procuring employment for it in the transit countries, while denying it any employment in our own country," Herzl wrote,[12] adding that:

The property-owners will come over to our side. Both the process of expropriation and the removal of the poor must be carried out discreetly and circumspectly. Let the owners of immovable property believe that they are cheating us, selling us things for more than they are worth. But we are not going to sell them anything back.[13]

And today, following the forced displacement of the Palestinian people, Israel is starving the refugees who ended up in the Gaza Strip. This starvation policy was summed up by Dov Weisglass, an adviser to then Israeli Prime Minister Ehud Olmert. "The idea is to put the Palestinians on a diet, but not to make them die of hunger," he said.[14] Consequently, the Israeli Ministry of Defense conducted a study of the nutritional needs of Palestinians in Gaza, so as to cap food imports into the blockaded area. Titled "Food Consumption in the Gaza Strip—the Red Lines," it is a detailed study of how many calories Palestinians need to consume to avoid malnutrition. By looking at what food can be produced within the besieged strip, it then determined what absolutely must be allowed in. The study calculated that 106 food trucks should cross into Gaza five days a week. This number, which was not met for years, is much smaller than the 400 food trucks a day that brought in food before the blockade.[15]

Much has been written about the water apartheid in Palestine today, a human rights violation that dates to 1967, when Israel occupied East Jerusalem, the West Bank, and the Gaza Strip. Shortly after that conquest and the ensuing illegal occupation, Israel consolidated complete control over all water resources and water distribution infrastructure. In November 1967, it issued a military order stating that Palestinians cannot construct any water extraction systems without a permit from Israel—permits that Israel systematically denies them. Palestinians are also denied access to the Jordan River and any fresh springs anywhere in the West Bank; and they are denied permits to deepen existing wells and drill new ones. Israeli settlers, on the other hand, face no restrictions on their water consumption, enjoying swimming pools, access to natural watering holes and fresh springs, and profiting from farming in well-irrigated fields, while Palestinian taps run dry. The disparity is visually jarring: in one instance, a mere barbed wire fence separates a field between a Palestinian family and an Israeli settler family. The Palestinian side is barren, parched; the Israeli side is lush. Overall, Israelis consume an average of 300 liters of water per person per day, while some Palestinians are restricted to 20 liters, well below the World Health Organization's recommended 100 liters per person per day.[16] All reports about the water crisis for Palestinians in the homeland agree that the cause of the problem is not water scarcity, but unequal distribution, with Israelis enjoying 85 percent of groundwater resources available in the West Bank.

As a result of this water theft, in the Jordan Valley, for example, settlers can grow profitable produce that consumes large quantities of water, such as bananas and citrus fruit, while Palestinians have had to limit themselves to a much smaller variety of vegetables that require little watering: eggplant, zucchini, and squash.[17] Citrus is failing in Palestinian fields, and thriving in neighboring fields tended by Israeli settlers, not because the Palestinians do not know how to tend to a crop they've grown for thousands of years, but because they do not have access to their own water. Besides diverting water from Palestinian aquifers toward Israeli cities and agricultural fields, Israel has created sterile "security zones" around the apartheid wall itself and surrounding the Gaza Strip. These "security zones" are regularly sprayed with herbicides, to prevent any growth that might facilitate Palestinian "infiltration" into Zionist held territory. In the Gaza Strip, the Coastal Aquifer, Gaza's only water source, is polluted by over-pumping and wastewater and seawater contamination. The fact that Palestinians cannot even repair the collapsing infrastructure is, again, an unnatural disaster, fully manufactured by Israel which does not allow into the Gaza Strip the materials needed for repair and maintenance. Mni Wiconi, Lakota for "water is life," is particularly applicable to this region, with its unsustainably dense human population, itself a result of displacement by Zionist settler colonialism.

And whereas climate change has greatly impacted all countries in the Mediterranean region, Palestine's woes are further aggravated by the colonizers' early desire to transform it into a different country. Indeed, like the Europeans who sought to shape Turtle Island into their image, the Zionists were also determined to change Palestine's landscape, from sparsely treed hills and valleys into the dense European forests they were leaving behind. The Zionists claimed they were "making the desert bloom." But Palestine did not respond well to that foreign interference. Wildfires have engulfed the tormented land for many years now, burning hottest and most out of control precisely in the pine forests planted by the Israelis to cover up, literally, the long-standing Palestinian stewardship of the land.

In the summer of 2021, for example, wildfires engulfed a dozen towns around Jerusalem, revealing the landscaped terraces Palestinians had tended for centuries, before the Zionist settlers uprooted the grapevines and olive trees. Many Palestinians commented that the fires were cleansing, purgative, as they took away the forests that had been forcefully imposed upon the native landscape. Many noted that "nature knows best." These forest fires are now almost an annual occurrence in Palestine, notably in the north, where Israel first transformed Palestinian villages and orchards into colonial forests celebrating the European settlers' background.

The colonizers' ravaging of Palestine is as old as their appropriation of the land. This is because the early Zionist settlers were intent on literally "setting down roots" in the land of Palestine, after ethnically cleansing it of its Palestinian people. The Jewish National Fund's "Plant a tree in Israel" program has been widely popular among Jews and Zionists globally since Theodor Herzl first launched it in 1901, with the little blue "pushke" box its most recognizable symbol. In 2020, the Jewish National Fund (JNF) boasted that it has planted more than 185 million trees, creating 280 forests and over 1,000 parks in the once sparsely treed land. Like Mount Rushmore in the Dakota sacred Black Hills, the Zionist forests are symbolic of colonial conquest: the very first JNF-planted forest was named the Theodor Herzl Forest, in honor of the father of Zionism. Another JNF forest is named "Balfour Forest," a tribute to Lord Balfour, who promised European Jews a homeland in parts of Palestine.

But Palestine is not European, and the JNF's commitment to "combat desertification," as the organization describes its program, proved to be an over-reach. Today, the JNF openly admits that it directs much of the money donated toward planting trees into other forest-related measures, including firefighting, and preventative measures such as chopping down trees to create firewalls. Yet the Zionist ambition to transform "arid Palestine" into "green Israel" still holds sway among the donors, who would rather fancy they are planting trees, not thinning forests. One of the common Zionist platitudes—as patently false as the claim that Palestine was "a land without people for a people without a land"—is that Israelis "made the desert bloom." Instead, within a few decades of their deliberate attempt to transform the country, they have made the desert burn.

Because the olive tree has long been symbolic of the Indigenous Palestinian presence, the JNF plants mostly pine trees, which do not carry a Palestinian political meaning. Hundreds of thousands of pine trees were planted in the desert, where only a few thorny bushes had earlier grown, necessitating the diversion of water from its natural paths to irrigate them. Pine seeds are easily dispersed, by wind or fire, and saplings grew in open areas, where they took over the previously barren space. Trees are nature's "green lung," generating oxygen and filtering pollutants. However, following massive and deadly wildfires in northern Israel, environmental studies have shown that the Zionist afforestation project contributed to environmental devastation. Ecologists today are recommending that Israelis plant fewer trees and limit themselves to replanting with native trees.[18] This is because the new Israeli forests were causing more warming than cooling, as their dense tree canopies absorb solar radiation, whereas the lighter colors of the native desert plants had once reflected the sun's heat away from the soil. Global warming certainly plays a major role in the overall temperature elevations around the world, including historic Palestine. Yet an Indigenous people attuned to the land would have tended it more carefully, seeking to preserve rather than transform it. Instead, the JNF's determination to "make the desert bloom" has been detrimental to Palestine's very nature, and its soil, which once sustained the people. Where once there was sustainable biodiversity, Israel supplanted a monoculture of pine trees. The very geography of Palestine today shows the ugly face of apartheid: recently planted "forests" within the 1948 borders, irrigated by water from diverted aquifers under parched Palestinian fields, and strips of bare land heavily sprayed with herbicides surrounding the majority-Palestinian areas.

Israel gets away with its many egregious crimes thanks to its very well-oiled propaganda machine. In addition to "redwashing," its claim to indigeneity, and "pinkwashing," its claim to being gay friendly, Israel has been engaging in "greenwashing," the appeal to environmentalists and animal rights activists. Thus, it actively touts its vegan-friendly population, as veganism has a much smaller environmental footprint than an animal-based diet. With 5 percent of Israelis reportedly vegan, Israel now prides itself on being a "vegan nation," and of course, uses that relatively high figure to greenwash murder—of humans. And as with pinkwashing, Global North liberals uncritically believe the Israeli propaganda. PETA (People for the Ethical Treatment of Animals) regularly publishes gushing praise of Israel on its website, calling it "the vegan capital of the world," completely skipping over the fact that Israel regularly engages in brutalization of Palestinians, while Israeli settlers frequently attack Palestinian farms in the West Bank, spitefully uprooting orchards and killing sheep with complete impunity. The *Vegetarian Times*, a magazine with articles and recipes about vegetarianism and veganism, frequently features Palestinian recipes that it claims are Israeli, crediting the start-up nation for inventing what is in reality the centuries old sustainable diet of the Palestinian people, and thus contributing to Palestine's cultural erasure. And even National Public Radio had a report about the "morality" of the Israeli military, which accommodates the vegan lifestyle of soldiers not only by providing vegan meals, but also by providing wool-free berets, and leather-free belts and combat boots. Of course, just as anti-pinkwashing activists were quick to point out that a bullet shot by a trans soldier is as lethal as one fired by a straight homophobe, so it should be obvious that a bomb dropped on a Palestinian home by an Israeli with a "leather-free" hemp belt will inflict as much harm on children huddled in that home as one dropped by a soldier who just polished off a bloody steak dinner. Indeed, it is hard to conceive of vegan soldiers who reconcile their care not to harm animals with their willingness to kill humans, yet this is one more of the incongruities of Zionism, as articulated by Omer Yuval, the Israeli soldier who first organized for vegan offerings in the Israeli Occupation Forces: "I believe that the vegan reform in the IDF is paving the way for an even more moral army," he said.[19]

Food Sovereignty Is National Sovereignty

Disasters discriminate. No analysis of the crises facing disenfranchised communities would be complete without a discussion of the rapidly cascading consequences, for these communities, of the environmental devastation wreaked by profit-driven "development." Having discussed the harm colonizers have inflicted on nature and the environment in the lands they took over, I will now address some of the responses by Indigenous peoples. My focus will be on food sovereignty, which is directly related to land access and cultural preservation.[20] The importance of local food for overall well-being is best illustrated in the common greeting throughout Southeast Asia, "have you eaten rice yet?" the equivalent of "how are you?" in English, which first emerged after the many wars and famines in that part of the world. And homemade food as an expression of love and community is quasi-universal, as evidenced by families getting together to cook on special occasions and reunions. It is also obvious in the "meal trains" that are organized when a person is sick, or bereaved, when community members take turns providing the needy person with homemade rather than store-bought meals.

The cultural erasure that accompanied conquest took the form of forcefully alienating the Indigenous people from their traditional diets. Therefore, decolonization necessarily involves preserving, reclaiming, and reviving these diets, which are organically connected to the land. Palestinian feminist scholar Lila Sharif's work, arguing that Palestinians everywhere sustain their attachment to the homeland through practices linked to the olive tree, is a valuable contribution to the study of decolonial practices. As an estimated 80 percent of small-scale farming and family cooking globally is done by women, food sovereignty directly empowers women, just as its loss negatively impacts them. To quote LaDuke again: "*Native women are here, and we birthed this place. We created the agrobiodiversity of 8,000 varieties of corn, and a multitude of beans, squash and melon varieties that are now touted by big agriculture and the foundation.*"[21]

In Palestine, women have historically foraged for the bounty of herbs and leafy greens that are an important part of Palestinian cuisine, and which provided them the means to secure social and economic independence. They are heavily involved at all stages of agriculture, as growers, harvesters, processors, and traders. Today, about a third of women in the West Bank are the only income-earners in their households. Going out in small groups to the fields at dawn, they expertly gather seasonal herbs, making sure they leave roots and seeds behind, to ensure the next season's harvest. They are finely attuned to the short-lived seasons that make for the hyper seasonal culinary calendar—blink and you miss it. I have often visited my mother and requested dishes that she told me I had just missed by weeks, or that would be available if only I stayed an additional two weeks. Khubbeizeh (mallow) grows between the months of February and May, zaatar (hyssop) and hummeid (bitter dock) leaves must be picked before the plant flowers in the summer heat, hindbeh (dandelion), a leafy green which happens to be one of my favorites, is fortunately available for many months each year. Akkoub (gundelia) is a thistle-like delicacy only harvestable for a very brief period in late winter or early spring, when the stem is still tender, before the seed pods have fully dried out. Palestinians know this and are careful not to over-forage. Many of the foragers also carefully spread the immature seed pods in the harvested areas, knowing from experience that these will eventually dry out, albeit not on the plant itself, and bloom again the following year. Akkoub is, after all, a perennial plant that has grown in Palestine for thousands of years—folklore has it that its seed pods were used to make Jesus' crown of thorns.

Palestinian women's foraging is unlike commercial farming, which involves the hoarding of seeds and operates year-round with greenhouses and produce at various stages of germination and growth, because heaven forbid we should not have mushrooms in August, or zucchini in January. Mostly, Palestinian women use the wild herbs for their own cooking, and on bountiful days, they sell what they have foraged at the local market. These plants secure their sustenance, yet the Israeli Nature and Parks Authority has banned foraging, under the pretense of "conservation." Palestinians view the ban as an affront to their identity and nationhood. It is ironic indeed that a country that spitefully uproots ancient olive trees, and sprays entire fields with herbicides to keep them barren for "security" reasons, is nevertheless supposedly concerned about the fate of plants that Palestinians cherish and have sustainably harvested for millennia.

Understandably, La Via Campesina (LVC) has always centered ending gender violence in its work and, in 2017, asserted itself as a feminist movement. Today, there are numerous food-, water-, and agriculture-related initiatives that are sprouting across Turtle Island, in Palestine and its diaspora, a majority of which are women-led. But just as not every woman is a feminist, so not every feminist is a woman. By looking at some of Palestinian agricultural centers today, we can get an overview of the feminist decolonial vision behind these initiatives, with the many life-affirming social and health benefits they produce.

First, a definition of food sovereignty is appropriate. The concept of "food sovereignty" was first launched onto the world stage outside the World Food Summit in Rome in 1996 by La Via Campesina, an international peasants' movement that took to the streets of Rome asserting that there could be no food security without food sovereignty. La Via Campesina centers "the struggle for land, justice, equality and to eradicate all forms of *gender discrimination and violence*" (emphasis in original).[22] The movement has been at the forefront of integrating an analysis of women's circumstances within the food sovereignty movement from its nascent days, as it repeatedly made demands for economic autonomy, access to land, and equal status for all, always specifying that women suffer specific forms of gender violence as rural, peasant women. At the 2013 LVC annual conference in Jakarta, Indonesia, the Women's Assembly started working on a proposal for "peasant, popular feminism" and, in 2017, LVC affirmed itself as a feminist movement. In November 2021, LVC released its graphic book, *The Path of Popular and Peasant Feminism in La Via Campesina*, available online in many languages. Like many other Global South groups, LVC has had to explain its own understanding of feminism, reclaiming it from white liberal women, stating:

> In the early days of the movement, peasant women did not consider themselves feminists but advocated for women's struggles. Working on gender in LVC has allowed us to move forward the debate and open spaces for women, and later, to talk about feminism.[23]

LVC then defines feminism as "a broad political strategy of structural transformation because violence and inequality are structural problems."[24]

Food sovereignty, which is directly connected to agency and access to land, is a decolonial move. This is because, as scholar-activist Raj Patel argues, it is possible to have "food security" even in a dictatorship. "The idea of food security is entirely compatible with a dictatorship— as long as the dictator provided vouchers for McDonald's and vitamins, a country could be said to be 'food secure'," Patel wrote.[25] He continues:

> Admittedly, this is an extreme example, but the history of the world food system is one of a few elites in a handful of countries telling the world how it was going to eat, and how best to feed itself. Today, these elites aren't dictators in third world countries. Today's architects of the food system are policy makers in institutions like the World Bank, the US Department of Agriculture and the European Commission, from where they write the food policy that affects the rest of the planet.[26]

But Patel need not have come up with the "extreme example" of a dictator providing vouchers for McDonald's: in Palestine, the dictators, the "architects of the food system" are the Israeli government officials who determine what diet is sufficient to keep Palestinians barely alive in the Gaza Strip. In the West Bank, the dictators and architects of the food system are Israel's Nature and Parks Authority, a "conservation" organization which has banned foraging for wild herbs and plants in what it calls an environmental move, which Palestinians view as purely political—these plants, like the olive tree, define Palestine's cultural heritage. Food sovereignty, then, unlike food security, involves questions of culture, power, identity, ecology, and land.

"Food sovereignty is tribal sovereignty," argues Indigenous environmentalist and nutritionist Valerie Segrest, who lives on the Muckleshoot reservation. In 2010, the Muckleshoot bought 30 acres of land which they dedicated to a food sovereignty project meant to empower the entire community. In *Choctaw Women in a Chaotic World: The Clash of Cultures in the Colonial Southeast,* author Michelene Pesantubbee discusses how women were responsible for tending the fields and growing the food in many nations where agriculture, rather than hunting or fishing, was the major source of food production.[27] This responsibility gave them significant social standing within their communities, but also with outsiders seeking to interact with these nations. The loss of land was thus accompanied by a loss of social status for women—a phenomenon further aggravated by the patriarchy the colonizers forced upon the Indigenous nations. Additionally, obtaining local food, which one has grown in a traditional manner, gave Indigenous peoples a deep understanding of the land and a strong connection to it. That connection was lost as they started purchasing non-local food from a store. Reviving small-scale agriculture, then, also helps reclaim one's heritage, even one's language, as that language has the correct words for grains or cooking methods that do not exist in the colonizer's language.

When they were forced onto reservations, the Indigenous were also limited almost exclusively to a European diet based on white flour, sugar, salt, lard, and dairy. With poverty and food stamps came "mystery meat" and "government cheese." "Mystery meat" is a disparaging term for the processed animal patty, nugget, or cake (especially Spam) which generally includes products from unidentifiable sources, frequently offal. It is much cheaper than a cut of meat and is generally served in prisons and school lunches. "Government cheese" is the processed, pasteurized dairy product generally available to people on welfare, social security beneficiaries, and food stamps recipients, and otherwise known as "American cheese." "American cheese" is cheaper to manufacture than traditional cheese and, so long as it contains 51 percent traditionally prepared cheese, can be processed with legally unregulated terms such as "pasteurized prepared cheese product." A diet of government cheese and mystery meat created the chronic epidemics of diabetes, obesity, and hypertension that plague Indigenous communities to this day. It also further disconnected the Indigenous from their heritage. As Chef Brit Reid, who lives on the Tulalip reservation, explained: "Just as you can't have Japanese cuisine without rice, you can't have Indian food without corn."[28] Yet, many Indigenous people today rely on sandwiches of white wheat bread with Spam and "government cheese" for their sustenance.

Meanwhile, in the blockaded Gaza Strip, the need to ensure "food security" has led to multinational organizations distributing flour, rice, sugar, and other shelf stable staples, taking away from traditional Palestinian cuisine, which relies on local, seasonal items. Food scarcity in the Gaza Strip today is such that the diet has changed from a meat- and fish-rich cuisine to one that is primarily vegan—not out of choice, but because of the weaponization of food and overall impoverishment of the captive society. The Gaza Strip has also seen a significant rise in cancer because of the excessive use of herbicide in the "border security zone," which Israel regularly sprays to keep it barren.[29] Israel is also one of the world's heaviest users of fertilizers and pesticides. When these exceed acceptable European standards, Israel dumps its rejected produce in Gaza, again contributing to the rise in cancer rates.

Yet it is the local, and seasonal, that continues to help Palestinian families in the West Bank and Gaza Strip, frequently providing women with the only option to earn any income at all. One example is the dates season in Gaza, during which hundreds of Palestinian women secure an income they cannot otherwise access. To avoid sinking into abject poverty, the women started harvesting dates, earning more in one season than during the rest of the year—should they even be able to find other employment. Working twelve hours a day, they pick, clean, and prepare the dates, sell some in the local market, and use the rest in pastries, jams, juices, and other traditional Palestinian recipes that are thus preserved and passed on to future generations. As they work together, these women are also empowered, finding solace in each other's company. Palestinian women throughout Palestine today are frequently the only breadwinner in their households, due to Israel's killing, maiming, or imprisoning of their husbands and sons, and the crushing unemployment rates. Chef Leila El-Haddad has documented many of their stories in The Gaza Kitchen, a storyteller's cookbook par excellence, couching personal and family stories in the broader social and economic context of living in a besieged strip.[30] Similarly, Vivien Sansour uses her food offerings in "The Traveling Kitchen," a mobile restaurant out of her car, as a catalyst to launch conversations about cultural heritage and biodiversity. Sansour, founder of the Palestine Heirloom Seed Library, is known as the "seed queen of Palestine," because of her commitment to preserve threatened food plant varieties in Palestine and around the world.

The weaponization of food is not limited to the Gaza Strip. Israel also routinely dumps its surplus produce in the West Bank in order to undermine Palestinian farming, already threatened by settler attacks. These settler attacks themselves are timed around the harvest times, primarily of grapes and olives, and are intended to destroy Palestinians' economic lifelines: an estimated 80,000 to 100,000 Palestinian extended families rely on the olive harvest as their sole source of income. This is why Palestinians fully understand that farming is resistance. Many are investing in environmentally friendly, organic, Indigenous agriculture, and in so doing are protecting the land and reclaiming their identity. Among these, the Palestine Institute for Biodiversity and Sustainability (PIBS), founded in 2008 by Dr. Mazin Qumsiyeh, plays a critical role in preserving Palestinian culture, agricultural knowledge, and traditions, while educating youth about responsible interaction with the environment. The PIBS has created numerous educational resources geared toward children, including colorful posters and animated games. Qumsiyeh has also produced an activist's toolkit, and the Institute runs numerous workshops and has regular opportunities for volunteers. Defying all the challenges of a brutal military occupation, water apartheid, economic strangulation, settler attacks, and a forced influx of Israeli and other foreign produce, small community-supported agricultural farms, as well as farmers' markets, are popping up across the West Bank, creating spaces for community, seed sharing, and mutual support.

Food-Fueled Social Justice

To regain food sovereignty, Indigenous chefs have eliminated ingredients introduced by the colonizers. "The Sioux Chef" collective, for example, completely eliminated wheat, dairy, soy, cane sugar, pork, and chicken, from their menu. North American Indigenous food is naturally dairy free and gluten free, and by "decolonizing" the kitchen, the Sioux Chef are also helping reduce diabetes and obesity among Indigenous folks. "The Sioux Chef" are a team of Anishinaabeg, Mdewakanton Dakota, Navajo, Northern Cheyenne, Oglala Lakota, Sisseton Wahpeton Dakota chefs and food preservationists, and also run NATIFS, the Native American Traditional Indigenous Food Systems, which focuses on improving access to traditional food throughout tribal communities in Turtle Island. Their vision hinges on an understanding that "Reclamation of ancestral education is a critical part of reversing the damage of colonialism and forced assimilation, and food is at the heart of this reclamation."[31]

Exiled Palestinians, however, face a different challenge. The need to reproduce Palestinian culture in the diaspora, where many of the seasonal, local greens are not available, has opened up unique opportunities to be innovative, producing hybrid products that remain faithful to the homeland—its spices, aromas, and flavors—while incorporating compatible ingredients from the diaspora. And to counter the overall Palestinian experience of dispossession, disenfranchisement, and discrimination, Palestinian cooking has taken on the additional flavor of social justice, creatively mixed with the flavors of the land of exile. In New York, for example, Chef Nasser Jaber, originally from Ramallah, explains that he does not feel the need to be fully faithful to traditional Palestinian food, reproducing it authentically, because others are doing that, and he prefers to look forward, not just to the past. "There's enough people preserving the cuisine, and the history of the cuisine, but who thinks about the future of the cuisine? Why should the cuisine remain the same?" Jaber asked, explaining that he feels it is his role to "take the cuisine forward."[32] Jaber is co-owner, with Daniel Dorado, of the highly successful Migrant Kitchen. Having experienced homelessness and debt himself, prior to The Migrant Kitchen, Jaber donates generously to the needy. In the summer of 2020, at the height of the COVID-19 pandemic in his adopted city of New York, Jaber and his crew were preparing and offering 6,000 free halal meals a day to frontline workers, homeless shelters, and domestic abuse shelters. The meals are delivered across the city in vans with "Black Lives Matter" and "Palestinian Lives Matter" decals. Before the pandemic, Jabber was already combining food with activism, as he hosted the "Displaced Kitchens," which gave refugees an opportunity to cook and share their stories to guests paying an average of 100 dollars a seat, with the proceeds going to refugees. Jaber has since opened operations in Lebanon, and he plans to build sustainable farms in Palestine, Syria, and Yemen, among other disaster-hit countries, all with a focus on feeding the poor, refugees, and displaced people.

Another diaspora Palestinian chef who centers social justice in her work is Reem Assil, owner of Reem's in Oakland, California. Assil launched her cooking through La Cocina program, a women's food incubator, by selling baked goods at a farmers' market. Assil was a community and labor organizer before becoming a chef, and chose to serve up a side of politics alongside her baked goods. The motto of her restaurant is "Where the man'ousheh meets the movement." A man'ousheh is an Arabic flatbread traditionally topped with a mix of dried herbs and olive oil, but Assil has elevated this basic street food by adding numerous additional topping options. Her restaurant in Oakland, which has shifted its focus to catering and wholesale orders since the pandemic, was famous for its mural of Rasmea Odeh, the Palestinian political prisoner who was tortured in Israeli jails, then deported to Jordan from the USA, where she had lived for many years upon her release from Israeli detention, and where she organized immigrant women. A smaller mural was that of Oscar Grant, the 22-year-old Black man murdered by police at the Fruitvale train station across from Reem's. Assil is deeply aware of the significance of her geographical location—one of the most diverse areas in the USA—and is intentional about hiring very locally (most of her employees live within walking distance of the restaurant), and majority women of color. Like Jabber, she too is an innovator, fusing Arabic food with the bounty of California's culinary traditions. The restaurant's website lists the establishment's three core values as community building, social justice, and sustainability. Specifically, the website explains that the restaurant seeks to create "a thriving local ecosystem by hiring and sourcing locally, minimizing our carbon footprint, and partnering with other local businesses that are aligned with our vision and values."[33] Reem's is worker-owned and offers its employees a living wage—something that is the exception, rather than the norm, in a cut-throat industry still dominated by white men.

Numerous other diaspora Palestinian ventures in Turtle Island also focus on community empowerment, including supporting impoverished Palestinians in the homeland. What is noteworthy about these Diaspora initiatives is how grounded they are in the need to give back to the community, of Palestinians generally, but also, of the oppressed, the underserved. For Palestinians, then, food sovereignty is two-pronged. In the homeland, the understanding that farming is resistance sustains families as they persist in tending the land that has long defined them. In the global diaspora, Palestinians are fighting cultural erasure and appropriation, even as they innovate on traditional dishes by adding a touch of fusion to these. Restaurants such as the Migrant Kitchen and Reem's proudly offer Palestinian staples "with a twist," as they incorporate local ingredients or global influences into their menu. Allies can support Palestinian food sovereignty by recognizing the Palestinian identity of the many dishes that pre-date the establishment of Israel, which now claims these dishes as Israeli cuisine. They can expose Israel's greenwashing. And most importantly, they should work to dismantle Zionism, because colonialism is incompatible with healthy living.

From Turtle Island to Palestine, the Indigenous people of the land have long had a respectful approach to the land that sustains them. They have not tried to shape it to reflect them, nor have they transformed it to remind them of their origins elsewhere. Similarly, from Turtle Island to Palestine, the Indigenous have not engaged in scorched earth strategies to optimize short-term resource extraction. Rather, they view themselves as springing from the land and as its stewards. In the Americas, the creation stories of many Indigenous nations view them as "people of the corn," created from the grain that is native to the land. Indigenous farming also relies on complementarity and intrinsic sustainability, as illustrated by the traditional planting of the "three sisters"—corn, beans, and squash—in clear contrast to the large-scale monocultures scarring the continent today. In Palestine, the people's identification with their land is best expressed by Fatima Breijeh, a woman from Ma'sara, Bethlehem, who noted:

> Our roots are fixed here. We, this land, this land, we are from this land. Look at the earth, at the soil; you will find it's our color. Every blade of grass, we know. They do not know anything. They only know to carry weapons and to steal—to steal water, to steal the blessings of our land—everywhere.[34]

In the first part of this chapter, I focused on the violence inflicted upon the land by the colonizers to emphasize the need for land restitution in decolonization. Today, Indigenous nations around the world are acutely aware of the urgency to heal the earth—literally—while engaging in decolonial struggles. Whether in the Gaza Strip, where food scarcity and water pollution are an Israeli-made catastrophe, or in the Navajo Nation, where one-third of Navajo families do not have running water in their homes, the Indigenous people suffer the most devastation; they are also the communities actively engaged in creating the solution. The movement to restore the land to its rightful owners would also restore dignity to the dispossessed and displaced Indigenous nations, allowing them to revive and reclaim their cultural heritage. It would ensure the essentials of dignified life: housing, food sovereignty, clean air and water, and personal safety. And where the settlers have tried to impose human and agricultural monocultures, the Indigenous have responded with their insistence on biodiversity as essential for survival. Today, the buffalo have come back from the brink of extinction, Palestinian chefs in exile are feeding their host communities, and Palestinian children in the homeland are learning to enjoy the land's seasonal offerings.

Sustainability. Community. Agency. Social Justice. Nourishment. These values are grounded in a feminist decolonial worldview that does not aspire to a trip into outer space, but rather, values life on this earth. Because, as Palestine's poet Mahmoud Darwish put it, "We have, on this land, that which makes life worth living."[35]

5

A Global Intifada

A Killer Alliance

On May 14, 1948, President Harry Truman went against the advice of many of his White House staff when he recognized Israel as a legitimate Jewish state within eleven minutes of its creation, thereby becoming the first world leader to do so. Since then, the rote repetition, by every US president and most US politicians, that "Israel is our closest strategic ally in the region," while it may sound formulaic at this point, is actually revealing of the American reliance on Israel's contributions to the USA: the billions of dollars the USA gives Israel every year are earmarked for Israel's military, precisely because Israel is an outpost of American interests in the region. The US–Israeli relationship was aptly described in 1986 by then Senator Joe Biden, who told the Senate:

> It's about time we stop apologizing for our support for Israel. There's no apology to be made. It is the best three-billion-dollar investment we make. If there weren't an Israel, the United States of America would have to invent an Israel to protect her interests in the region.[1]

That relationship is enacted in the financial, military, and diplomatic aid that the USA offers Israel, not as the idiosyncratic fancy of one or another president, but consistently, since the USA first grasped the power and importance of Israel in the region. It is important to note that Israel is required to spend most of the money it gets from the USA on US weapons purchases—effectively looping it back into US coffers, and more specifically, the military industrial complex. Meanwhile, Israel relies on the USA to be the outside power, the "iron wall"

Jabotinsky had declared was necessary to subdue the Palestinians. In his seminal essay, discussed in Chapter 1, "Settler Colonialism and Indigenous Resistance," Jabotinsky had written:

Zionist colonisation must either stop, or else proceed regardless of the native population. Which means that it can proceed and develop only under the protection of a power that is independent of the native population—behind an iron wall, which the native population cannot breach.[2]

He immediately went on to explain that the "iron wall" would be an outside power, and presumed this would be Great Britain, which first promised parts of Palestine to the European Zionists. As England eventually stepped away from this role, the USA took over as patron of the new country. Jabotinsky writes:

That is our Arab policy; not what we should be, but what it actually is, whether we admit it or not. What need, otherwise, of the Balfour Declaration? Or of the Mandate? Their value to us is that outside Power has undertaken to create in the country such conditions of administration and security that if the native population should desire to hinder our work, they will find it impossible.[3]

What has grown to become a reciprocal relationship is seen in the way that the USA adopts techniques and technologies of repression first tested by Israel against the Indigenous Palestinian population. This is amply evident today in the way the US practices, against communities residing within its borders, the policing, surveillance, racial profiling, counter-insurgency methods, and hypermilitarization that Israel has perfected against the Palestinian people. It is now quite common to see military equipment—armored personnel carriers, Humvees, assault rifles, and other trappings of urban warfare—deployed in American city streets to quash protests against murderous police racism, just as Israel uses its military powers and personnel to subdue Palestinians in the West Bank and Gaza Strip.

Here, however, it must be noted that the USA did not "learn" racism or violence from Israel. The USA pre-dates Israel by centuries, and the North American colonies were founded on racism, first and foremost against the Indigenous peoples of this continent, then against Africans and their descendants. The history of racist American policing is part and parcel of the history of this country. Suggesting that Israel, and the joint trainings of US and Israeli security forces, are the source of racism in US police departments is anachronistic and shifts the blame away from the USA. It cannot be overemphasized that the US police forces have been racist since their very inception, with many American police forces in southern cities having their origin as slave patrols hunting down runaway enslaved people. Meanwhile, in northern cities such as Boston, the mandate of the colonial police forces, from the very beginning, was always to protect the "property" of the wealthy—namely, whites—and to suppress political and labor riots by the poor and downtrodden, mostly Irish and Italian immigrants, racialized and viewed as a threat to the Protestant ethics of the early colonies. This racism is one of the "shared values" that made the USA look to the upstart Israeli state as a security ally. Racism is violence, and police brutality in the USA is centuries old, certainly older than Israel itself. Considering the many denunciations made in the past few years that the training of US police forces in Israel has led to the violent encounters we see across the USA today, I find it critically important to emphasize that US police racism, and brutality, long pre-date these joint trainings, which only started in 2002, as part of counterterrorism measures following the 9/11 2001 attacks.

One of the Israeli companies that train US security forces, for example, is called "Instinctive Shooting International," and promotes itself as setting "unmatched new standards" in tactical and counterterror courses. "Instinctive Shooting International," now American-owned, started out in 1999 as an Israeli company, run by Israeli veterans, to train US security forces in Israeli practices that are "proven, effective, and field tested." The "field" where these practices were tested is, of course, Palestine.[4]

In addition to the joint US–Israeli weapons training, many US police officers are trained in Krav Maga, the Israeli hand-to-hand combat style which is the official self-defense technique of the Israeli army. Even though it is derived from martial arts, boxing, and wrestling, Krav Maga is neither considered an art nor a sport, and as such does not concern itself with the safety of the victim, aiming instead at inflicting maximum pain, quickly and efficiently. One website promoting the fighting technique states: "All styles of punching, kicking, chokes, and take-downs are employed with the aim of neutralizing the enemy in the shortest amount of time possible. Krav Maga has no limitations. Groin, eyes, throat, and face are all fair game."[5] The promotional website explains that there are no Krav Maga competitions, as the risk would be too great for the participants, since:

> Perhaps the most unique aspect of Krav Maga is the emphasis on aggressiveness—it teaches you to stick to the goal no matter what, even when it is hard, even when you feel you have nothing left. Krav Maga has a no compromising attitude towards the enemy. The goal is to neutralize the enemy; the specific technique does not matter.[6]

Such exceedingly dangerous combat techniques are now finding their way into US police training, likely leading to an increase in fatal encounters between US police and unarmed citizens. The McKinney, Texas police officer who slammed 15-year-old Dajerria Becton face-first into the ground, pulling her by the hair as he planted his knee on her back, was listed as an instructor at a fitness center where he "now exclusively trains in Krav Maga, Arnis, and ground fighting."[7] Some people familiar with Krav Maga believe they also recognized its influence in Derek Chauvin's 2020 murder of George Floyd, resulting from a "knee-to-neck" maneuver that led to his asphyxiation.

It is important to note that even as national and international attention is understandably directed at US police violence against Black men, Native Americans remain the racial group most disproportionately killed by US police, as well as those most disproportionately incarcerated, generally serving longer sentences than other races for the same crimes, and serving the most life sentences of all race and ethnicities in the USA. This phenomenon does not receive enough coverage because, numerically speaking, Natives account for less than 2 percent of the US population, as compared to 13 percent for Black Americans. And while this "elimination of the native," through outright murder and life imprisonment, is a continuation of the genocide of the Indigenous peoples of this continent, today, it is also reflective of the militarization of US *police*, who are now doing what the US *army* had previously done. Urban warfare has been brought into the metropolitan cities, turning them into battlefronts, hence the currency of the image of "occupation forces" when militarized American police attack civilian protestors. Sadly, while the reported sexual abuse of gender-conforming cis men during arrest, or while in police custody, makes headline news, the assault, invasive searches, and humiliation of women, trans people, and gender non-conforming individuals is a pervasive phenomenon, but rarely raises eyebrows, as it is "business as usual," an enhanced manifestation of the rape culture pervasive in civilian society. Still, the gendered violence of the police against women of color, and gender-non-conforming individuals of color, has been documented by many anti-police groups, notably the grassroots collective INCITE! Feminists of Color Against Violence.[8]

Inter/Nationalism and the Global Intifada

The above discussion sought to provide context for the *militarization* of US police forces in connection with their joint trainings with Israeli security forces, while emphasizing that this training is in no way the source of US racism or violence. As Steven Salaita put it: "Israel is not merely an ally or client of the United States, but a profound component of its imperial practice."[9] Israel offers the USA "field-tested" military training that contributes to the hypermilitarization of US police, who now treat disenfranchised communities as enemies. Meanwhile, a radical popular uprising is afoot globally, in what I will term the "anticolonial boomerang effect," a coming together of oppressed communities against a common oppressor. The concept of the "imperial boomerang effect," upon which I base my own "anticolonial boomerang effect," was first articulated in the middle of the twentieth century to explain how "enlightened" European countries could embrace fascism. Political analysts were puzzled at how Germany, for example, so seamlessly shifted from the cultural renaissance of the Golden Twenties to the fascism of the 1930s and the horrors of the Holocaust. Others pointed out, however, that Hitler's Germany was not engaging in crimes that European powers had not committed elsewhere; the only difference being that these were now committed at home, in a "boomerang effect," rather than in the colonies.

The global uprising, or anticolonial boomerang effect, is brought about by those who have historically fallen at the intersection of the many oppressive systems both within their societies, and globally, and who have identified state-sanctioned murderously racist "law enforcement" as their common oppressor. It is no accident that the organizers of the new uprising, globally, are women of color, queers, immigrants, refugees, undocumented, Indigenous—the criminalized of the earth—united by an organic understanding of the commonality of their circumstances, and the need to rise together against such oppressive structures as militarism, heteropatriarchy, capitalism, racism, and colonialism. This is evident at multiple levels today, from Palestinians telling protestors in Ferguson, Missouri, how to protect themselves from tear gas, to the Movement for Black Lives embracing the Palestinian struggle, to the Red Nation collective declaring that "Palestine is the moral barometer of indigenous North America," to queers of all ethnicities organizing together to shut down pinkwashing events, to a delegation of Black, Indigenous, and women of color feminists endorsing BDS after a fact-finding trip to Palestine. The reciprocity is evident in collaborative ventures such as the video "When I See Them, I See Us," which features over sixty Black and Palestinian artists and activists highlighting challenges that both communities are confronting, including militarized policing and the prison industry.[10] And it is best articulated by Nadia Ben-Youssef, co-founder of the Adalah Justice Project, who explained "Our whole theory of change can be distilled as de-exceptionalizing

Israel–Palestine. I don't want more Palestinian rights activists. I want more human rights defenders."[11]

One of the many beautiful illustrations of the organic grasp of transnational struggle happened in 2016, when the first baby born at the Standing Rock Sioux Reservation, a Lakota child named Mni Wiconi, "water is life," was lovingly wrapped by her mother, Zintkala Mahpiya Wi Blackowl, Sky Bird Black Owl, in a Palestinian kuffiyeh.[12] Black Owl had taken her other four children to the camp where, because of her advanced pregnancy, she did not participate in frontline demonstrations. Steeped in Lakota tradition, Black Owl nevertheless chose to adorn her baby's basket with the traditional Palestinian scarf that has acquired a global political meaning and symbolism. Black Owl herself had earlier worn the kuffiyeh, which she later wrapped around her baby's basket, explaining that her giving birth is an act of resistance. "Having babies is my act of resistance; our reproductive rights as Native women have been taken away from us in so many ways. At one time, we were forcibly sterilized; assimilation has come down really hard on us."[13] From two continents away, Black Owl's words echo those of Fatima Breijeh, whom Palestinian chronicler Rima Najjar describes as "a Palestinian mother-earth figure." Breijeh, who has lost one son to Israel's violence, asserts: "I have decided to continue to resist until the last breath and to continue to urge people to resist and to teach my children to resist and to lay the foundation for this through their milk."[14]

We saw earlier how colonialism is threatened by Indigenous women's fertility, and seeks to control it in Palestine as it did in North America. Today, the global recognition that violence against society's most vulnerable is a structural problem is cementing the alliances between colonized and Indigenous peoples everywhere. Grounded in the indivisibility of justice, these alliances center gender oppression, with the understanding that liberating communities hinges on the liberation of women and queer members of those communities.

In this second half of this chapter, we look at how transnational and inter/national alliances are transforming popular resistance, as various marginalized groups that fall at the intersection of empire, structural racism, sexism, militarization, occupation, capitalism, and police violence, from Gaza to Standing Rock to Ferguson, are rising together in a global intifada: the "anticolonial boomerang effect." I borrow the term "inter/nationalism" from public intellectual Steven Salaita, whose brilliant book by this title is an extant analysis of the intersections and parallels between Palestine and Native America, from the early East Coast colonies to Hawaii. The slash in "inter/nationalism" foregrounds that while these joint struggles transcend boundaries, bringing people together from across the globe, they are nonetheless grounded in the concept of "nation" as indigeneity, rather than "country." With grass-roots joint initiatives happening all around the world, and becoming the norm rather than the exception, it is impossible to even list all the kinds of alliances that are forming, from labor, such as unionized dock workers in Seattle refusing to unload an Israeli cargo ship, to the local media in Arkansas, where a small publisher is suing the state over a pledge not to boycott Israel. Instead, I will focus on examples that uplift the reciprocity being practiced among marginalized communities, from Turtle Island to Palestine. I hope this small sampling will point to an appreciation of the myriad such initiatives emerging globally.

"I am Become a Palestinian"

Much has been said about the young Palestinians tweeting advice to Black protestors during the 2014 riots that erupted in Ferguson, Missouri, in the wake of the police murder of eighteen-year-old Michael Brown. Informed by decades of experience confronting the military juggernaut of their occupier, Palestinians told American protestors how to protect themselves from tear gas and the violence of riot police trained for warfare against unarmed civilians in the streets, rather than on a distant battlefront. "Run against the wind when you're being tear-gassed," Palestinians advised protestors in Ferguson. "Do not rub your eyes, do not wash them out with water," they offered, recognizing in the scenes from the Midwestern American city the violence that was their own daily reality. Shortly afterwards, in 2015, a large coalition of Black-led organizations and individuals from a total of twenty-five countries signed a "Black Solidarity with Palestine" statement in which they "reaffirmed solidarity with the Palestinian struggle and commitment to the liberation of Palestine's land and people."[15] The coalition articulates a deep understanding of the connections between the struggles of Palestinians and Blacks globally, as they write: "While we acknowledge that the apartheid configuration in Israel/Palestine is unique from the United States (and South Africa), we continue to see connections between the situation of Palestinians and Black people."[16] The signatories go on to explain that while the US and Israeli security forces would criminalize and brutalize Blacks and Palestinians, respectively, even if they had not trained together, the joint trainings are proof of the ideology shared by these oppressive forces. The statement then calls for "unified action against anti-Blackness, white supremacy, and Zionism."

In 2016, a year after that statement was issued, the Movement for Black Lives (M4BL), a sister organization to the Black Lives Matter movement, also affirmed its solidarity with Palestinians, and denounced the alliance between the USA and Israel. Their platform, "A Vision for Black Life," looks at the impact of this alliance both in the USA, where communities are deprived of much-needed funding that is diverted to Israel, and in Palestine, where that funding is then used by Israel to oppress Palestinians.[17]

Yet, as many scholars of social movements have noted, Black–Palestinian solidarity is not a recent phenomenon but can be traced to the anticolonial impulse that swept over the African continent, and its American Diaspora, as early as the middle of the twentieth century. Michael Fischbach writes that the first public pronouncement of Black support for the Palestinian cause was an essay penned by Ethel Minor, a young SNCC member, journalist, and organizer, and published in 1967 in the newsletter of the Student Nonviolent Coordinating Committee (SNCC). The essay was deeply critical of Israel, and of the US and British support for Zionism. Fischbach offers that this was "the event that first rocketed the Black Power movement into the American public's view in terms of black support for the Palestinians and the mixing of domestic racial identity with foreign policy."[18] SNCC, like most politicized Black groups, had developed a critical analysis of many global issues, including the anti-apartheid struggle in South Africa, the

Algerian Revolution, the Cuban Revolution, the crisis in the Congo, the Vietnam War, and Palestine. They regularly read and discussed Frantz Fanon's writings on colonialism. Fischbach also quotes prominent Black Power member Stokely Carmichael as being outraged at the alliance between Israel and South Africa, as he wrote: "I have to say, discovering that the government of Israel has been maintaining such a long, cozy, and warm relationship with the worst enemy of Black people came as a real shock. A kind of betrayal." Then, commenting on the attempt, even then, to censor criticism of Israel, Carmichael adds: "And hey, we weren't supposed to even *talk* about this? C'mon."[19] (emphasis in original)

Khury Petersen-Smith notes that, in the 1950s and 1960s, the Nation of Islam viewed the Arab world as a site of struggle against European imperialism. Malcolm X, whose politics were formed within the Nation of Islam, writes in his autobiography that Great Britain had helped "wrest Palestine away from the Arabs, the rightful owners."[20] And, in 1982, the connections between the Black and Palestinian struggles against violent supremacist powers were articulated again by June Jordan, following the massacres of Palestinians in the Sabra and Shatila refugee camps in Lebanon. The killings were perpetrated by Lebanese Phalangists, under the patronage of Israel—the Israeli Defense Minister at the time, Ariel Sharon, was found directly responsible for the massacres, which a United Nations commission later concluded constituted a form of genocide. Upon reading about these atrocities, Jordan, a black American poet, penned her powerful poem, "Moving Towards Home," where she identifies with the dispossessed, hounded, bereaved Palestinians, as she writes "I was born a black woman/ and now/ I am become a Palestinian." These lines later inspired Palestinian American poet Suheir Hammad to title her own 2010 poetry book *Born Palestinian, Born Black*, again making the connection between the struggles of the two communities.[21] That solidarity had long flowed both ways, as Angela Davis frequently points out, noting that when she was imprisoned in 1971, she received many letters from Palestinians.[22]

Black–Arab solidarity suffered a temporary setback in the immediate aftermath of the 2001 terror attacks, as Keeanga-Yamahta Taylor notes, when some Black Americans approved of the racial profiling of Arabs and Arab Americans. This rift, however, was short-lived: when the Patriot Act, passed in response to the 9/11 attacks, *sanctioned* the racial profiling of brown people, it normalized that of Blacks. Racial profiling had earlier been noted as an abuse of policing in the mid-1990s, following the 1994 Crime Bill, when organizers and activists first denounced the phenomenon of "driving while black." "Driving while black" was unofficially endorsed by a 1996 US Supreme Court ruling allowing police to pull over drivers for any traffic offense, with anecdotal evidence, later confirmed by an American Civil Liberties Union (ACLU) study, revealing that Blacks were disproportionately pulled over and searched. Within years, "flying while Arab" was a companion to "driving while black." Thus, the Patriot Act legitimized racial profiling and normalized surveillance, as it urged vigilante citizens to "see something, say something." As some Blacks who had temporarily distanced themselves from Arab Americans recognized this profiling that had long targeted their own communities, they once again grasped that they are in joint struggle with this criminalized community. Meanwhile, Palestinian activists like Linda Sarsour had long organized to denounce anti-Black racism, as well as Islamophobia. Sarsour had witnessed anti-Black racism as a teenager in the 1990s, when she attended John Jay High School in Brooklyn, where the student population was 90 percent Black and Latinx, and which she describes as "a barred school: all the windows had padlocked iron screens or vertical bars, and students were regularly stopped and frisked by cops outside the school long before 'stop and frisk' was an official New York Police Department policy."[23] "At John Jay I began to realize that my experience as a first generation Palestinian American Muslim was inextricably interwoven with the everyday reality of my Black and brown brothers and sisters in this country," Sarsour writes, again noting the fusion between the two struggles.[24]

Other prominent Black public intellectuals who have spoken out in support of Palestine include James Baldwin, Cornel West, Marc Lamont-Hill, bell hooks, Robin D.G. Kelley, Barbara Ransby, and many more. Specifically, Angela Davis recalls that the Palestinians who sent her letters when she was in prison recognized in her imprisonment, on political, racist charges, their own experience with arbitrary arrest and imprisonment by Israeli authorities. In all these cases, the solidarity between Black and Palestinian people hinges on a deep understanding that the struggle of these communities is against empire, racism, and supremacist violence. Black radicals view Palestine as a country colonized by the same racist forces that have occupied, unsettled, and oppressed Indigenous people and people of color from North America to Africa to Asia, and with which they identify as a minority living under occupation in North America, just as the Palestinians are living under occupation in their homeland, now known to the West as Israel.

The imperial violence has taken on different forms over the years, but is now looking more similar, from North America to Palestine, because of the joint trainings. And the "justice system" in both countries serves the supremacist ideology, as we see white supremacist and vigilante killers in the USA literally get away with murder, just as we see Israeli soldiers protecting the illegal settlers in Palestine. And both Palestinians in Palestine, and the various criminalized communities in Turtle Island, understand that just as the oppressor is united, from Israel to the USA, so the resistance to oppression must form a common front: joint struggle, not mere solidarity. This is one of the many manifestations of the global intifada, or the anticolonial boomerang effect.

Defiant Indigeneity

"We are not American. We are not American. We are not American," Haunani-Kay Trask repeated as she addressed a cheering crowd of Kanaka Maoli on January 17, 1993, the centennial of the US overthrow of Hawaii. And she insisted: "We will die as Hawaiians. We will never be Americans."[25] Trask's speech articulates the defiance that has long sustained native peoples globally in their rejection of their colonizers' rule. Indeed, when Patrick Wolfe wrote that settler colonialism is a *structure*, he meant to emphasize that it is an ongoing process, rather than a one-time event that happened and then concluded at a specific historic moment in the past. Settler colonialism must continue to engage in colonial violence, in displacement, land theft, cultural erasure, and killings, precisely because the colonized refuse to be conquered. This ongoing violence, decades after the onset of al-Nakba, is most obvious today in Israel's "Judaization" of Jerusalem, which necessitates the ethnic cleansing of long-time Palestinian residents so that more Jewish settlers can move into their homes. It is palpable in its desecration of the ancient Mamilla Cemetery, Jerusalem's oldest Muslim final resting place, so as to build the Simon Wiesenthal Center's "Museum of Tolerance" there. It is evident in the official promotion of the beauty of Israel's beachside atop the site of a Palestinian massacre at Tantoura. But it is just as pernicious in the less obvious (to some) ways that US national holidays persist in celebrating colonial conquest, and school curricula erase Critical Race Theory—the study of race-based resistance to systemic oppression—while embracing cosmetic multiculturalism—featuring enchiladas on school menus for Cinco de Mayo. And white men with dream catchers hanging from their rearview mirrors are still raping Indigenous women as part of the ongoing conquest of this continent.

Even the majority of those settlers who do acknowledge that harm has been done to the colonized find it virtually impossible to conceive of total land restitution—the end of the USA, or Israel. They view their buildings, institutions, social and cultural ways, their "facts on the ground," as here to stay, even if these have obliterated earlier buildings, institutions, social and cultural ways. But for the dispossessed Indigenous peoples globally, history is not linear, it is not necessarily "progress," and it is reversible. The Kanaka Maoli have not become American, and are seeking to regain collective sovereignty, that is, independence from the USA. The Navajo, Sioux, Mohawk, and Lenape remain Navajo, Sioux, Mohawk, and Lenape, living on Navajo, Sioux, Mohawk, and Lenape lands—albeit known to the settlers as Arizona, Dakota, New York, and New Jersey. And the Palestinians have not transformed into, and never will become, Israelis, even when some have Israeli citizenship. Indeed, the common use of quotation marks around the word Israel is a constant reminder that Palestinians do not recognize the legitimacy of that settler colonial country. And the Indigenous peoples, from Hawaii to Aoteaora to Palestine, want the land back, because they understand that their dispossession, with all its ill consequences to their communities and the entire globe, comes from the land theft which deprived them of the means to protect life on earth. Indeed, our very survival as a species depends upon returning the land to its rightful stewards, and those stewards' decolonial practices, as they abolish seed monopolies, big agriculture, imperial borders, and the pyrrhic Zionist desire to make the desert bloom.

One of the many ironies surrounding the question of Palestine in academia is the absence of that country from most postcolonial scholarship, even though the field of Postcolonial Studies owes its existence, to a significant extent, to the late Palestinian scholar Edward Said. By contrast, as Steven Salaita and Lila Abu-Lughod, among other scholars, have noted, Palestine has been central to the newly revitalized field of Indigenous and Settler Colonial Studies, which examines the ongoing colonization of Indigenous peoples, and their struggles for sovereignty and self-determination outside the framework of anticolonial national liberation.[26] The centrality of Palestine to Settler Colonial Studies in turn reveals the new analytical framework now operating in Palestinian organizing, which no longer aligns primarily with those countries that achieved the ouster of the European colonizer in the twentieth century, but rather with Indigenous and First Nations still living in the belly of the beast. Thus, whereas the discipline of "postcolonial studies" looks at the mostly nationalist struggles of the predominantly African and Asian countries for independence from such canonical imperial powers as England, France, and the Netherlands, Settler Colonial Studies looks at decolonial struggles to reclaim suppressed or appropriated cultures *within* empire. Again, this reflects the shift in Palestinian activism, which once sought to achieve liberation and a recognized nation state through armed struggle, and now aspires to autonomy, decolonization, and self-determination through global grassroots popular resistance, primarily BDS. The understanding is that decolonization will be achieved not through partition of the historic homeland, and the recognition of an amputated but "independent" Palestinian state, but rather, through the rethinking of citizenship, sovereignty, and nationhood, from the river to the sea and also beyond, in the global diaspora.

Palestinian thinkers have articulated extremely well-thought-out proposals for how to accomplish this, including Samir Abed-Rabbo's *One Democratic State*,[27] Mazin Qumsiyeh's *Sharing the Land of Canaan*,[28] Ali Abunimah's *One Country*,[29] and the excellent collection of essays edited by Laila Farsakh, *Rethinking Statehood in Palestine*.[30]

Thus we see that, at the academic level, the connections between Native Americans and Palestinians are articulated in the field of Settler Colonial Studies. At the grassroots level, the organic connections between these communities are collective, mostly women-led, and manifest in joint embraces of defiant indigeneity and decolonial praxis, from Hawaii to the Gaza Strip. This is happening spontaneously on an individual level, as in the case of Black Owl, who wrapped her newborn baby in a kuffiyeh, as well as among groups, as when a delegation from the Palestinian Youth Movement traveled to the Standing Rock reservation, to join the protests against the North Dakota Pipeline that would cut through sacred Siouxland and speed the ecological devastation of the reservation. Meanwhile, the Red Nation collective, one of the more radical Indigenous collectives "dedicated to the liberation of Native peoples from capitalism and colonialism," also stresses global decolonization, as it aligns with the dispossessed, displaced, and colonized everywhere, including in Palestine.[31]

The Red Nation's analysis is exemplary of inter/nationalism, as it is grounded in the local lived realities of the Indigenous peoples of Turtle Island, while remaining aware of the global manifestations of imperialism. "The police and border patrol tactics we are facing here are very much connected to global patterns of war, occupation, and border enforcement," they write. "We draw your attention to the collaboration between US police agencies and the Israeli occupation forces that displace, harass, and murder Palestinians in their homelands."[32] And like the Black radical organizers who understood that they are in joint struggle with the Palestinian people against the same enemy— state-sanctioned racism and dehumanization—the Red Nation collective also understands that the struggle of all Indigenous nations is one and the same. They write:

Look at Standing Rock in 2016 when Indigenous people defending their treaty lands were brutalized by the National Guard. ... Look at Hawai'i and Mauna Kea where Kanaka Maoli—Hawai'i's Indigenous people—continuously face violence from the US military, along with being arrested by police for protecting their sacred sites. ... Look at Palestine, surrounded by two of the largest US military aid recipients, Israel and Egypt. Look at Okinawa, where in early 2019, tens of thousands of Japanese citizens called for the closure of US military bases. Look at Guam. Look at Vietnam. Look at Bolivia. Look at the Philippines. Look at Afghanistan, Look at Iraq. The Indian Wars never ended, the United States simply fabricated new Indians—new terrorists, insurgents and enemies—to justify endless wars and endless expansions.[33]

The collective then states: "We owe it to our kin in the Global South to remember that our struggle for liberation is the same struggle they face."[34] This is the kind of transnationalism that was articulated in the middle of the twentieth century by Kwame Nkrumah, who insisted that the liberation of Ghana is meaningless unless it is linked with the total liberation of the African continent. It is the transnationalism of Nelson Mandela, who asserted, on the International Day of Solidarity with the Palestinian People, in 1997, that "we know too well our freedom is incomplete without the freedom of the Palestinians; without the resolution of conflicts in East Timor, the Sudan, and other parts of the world."[35] And it is the inter/nationalism of Steven Salaita, who maintains that: "Palestine can't be properly free while Hawaii is still occupied."[36]

The Indigenous liberation struggle has many fronts, as we saw in Chapter 4, and involves food sovereignty, which the Red Nation claims necessitates the abolition of borders. They explain that, historically, Indigenous peoples have preserved seeds by sharing them with neighboring communities, thus strengthening crop diversity that is currently threatened with extinction by big agriculture and food monopoly tycoons. "Imperial borders directly affect our trade and seed sharing with our relatives internationally that we have traditionally traded with," they write, as they discuss the high rates of food insecurity from Turtle Island to Palestine—especially in the Gaza Strip, where the imperial border is an apartheid wall choking a large concentration camp. Importantly, the Red Nation collective also discusses the gendered violence of settler colonialism, bringing attention to what they term the "genocide of MMIWG2S." And like Sarah Deer, and most Palestinian feminists, the collective asserts that this gendered violence is political, a direct result of colonialism, rather than cultural, inherent to the Indigenous communities' customs. The basic assumption in decolonial struggles is that the culture of the settler, the occupier, must be abolished, expelled from the psyche of the colonized, for it is that culture, and its internalization, that does the most harm to disenfranchised communities.

In other words, it is not only the concrete, physical structures of colonialism that must be abolished. Yes, the borders, prisons, "museums of tolerance" erected upon ancient cemeteries, playgrounds sprawled upon sites of massacres, and gargantuan portraits of white settler presidents sculpted into sacred Indigenous mountains, must go. More importantly, however, so must the toxicity that has poisoned many within the colonized communities. This decolonization of the mind is what would allow for the thriving of the most marginalized: the women, two-spirits, queers, and differently abled, who have always sustained us, and continue to lead us toward more equitable societies.

The late Palestine Liberation Organization (PLO) leader Yasser Arafat is known to have repeatedly asserted that the Palestinians "are not Red Indians," because in his mind, unlike the "Red Indians," Palestinians have not been wiped out, and continue to challenge the colonizer. Arafat's insistence, while he meant it as an affirmation that Palestinians have not been defeated, was sadly oblivious to the many decolonial initiatives of the Indigenous people of Turtle Island, whose own persistence long pre-dates Palestinian *sumoud*. Indeed, as Mohawk scholar Audra Simpson noted in a lecture she gave in Palestine, where she recognized the indigeneity of the Palestinian people, "We may well all be Red Indians." And we should be, because the only sustainable future is Indigenous.

Queers Against Imperial Homonationalism

Our third example of global intifada, or the anticolonial boomerang effect, looks at transnational queer alliances against homonormativity and empire. Because of their positionality always outside of hegemonic society's standards of acceptability, queers, especially diasporic queers of color, have long developed a political analysis that aligns with the "wretched of the earth," to use Fanon's canonical expression, or "les misérables," as James Baldwin called the Algerians in Paris. Before we look at these queer alliances, however, it may be useful to recall our discussion of pinkwashing in Chapter 3, "Social and Political Liberation." This is because pinkwashing would not be possible without homonormativity, which gives its blessing to privileged gays' access to upward social mobility and respectability. We saw how pinkwashing is the twenty-first-century manifestation of the Zionist colonialist narrative of bringing civilization to an otherwise benighted land—the myth of "mission civilisatrice" that nineteenth-century colonizers hoped would sanitize their violence. And just as the Zionist myth of "making the desert bloom" completely distorted the reality of the environmental devastation of Palestine, so pinkwashing distorts the reality of Israel's violence against all Palestinians, regardless of their sexuality. Specifically, denunciations of pinkwashing point to the fact that Israel is only "gay friendly" toward some of its own Jewish citizens, and the gay tourists it caters to. As far as Israel is concerned, Palestinian gays remain first and foremost Palestinian, and are thus barred from Israel's "friendliness." They are not spared the human rights violations that Israel subjects all Palestinians to: home demolitions, bombings, arbitrary arrests and extrajudicial executions, denial of the right of return if in the diaspora, etc. Gay Palestinians, then, are always outside of Israel's norms of acceptability. Even when some are extorted into serving their occupier, they remain other—racialized as outsiders, not "nationals" of the Jewish state.

Additionally, Israel prides itself on the fact that openly gay Israelis were able to serve in the army long before the USA, for example, dropped its ban on openly gay soldiers. This acceptance is an example of homonormativity: the participation of openly gay individuals in a country's military, while viewed as "equality" by many, is critiqued by radical queers as the gaining of access to an oppressive institution, rather than the dismantling of that institution. "Don't ask, don't tell," and its repeal, both *reform* the military, but they do not seek to abolish it. It remains an institution of death.

Homonormativity, then, is the normalization of some gay and lesbian individuals—generally white, cisgendered, and aspiring to a "normal" status, which they can attain—at the expense of the ongoing exclusion of others—mostly racialized queers who do not conform to society's acceptable standards. The term was coined by Jasbir Puar, who argues in *Terrorist Assemblages* that the inclusion of the "properly homo" subjects into the nation state depends specifically on distinguishing these assimilated individuals from the Orientalized "terrorist" bodies.[37] Homonormativity thus stresses the "proper homos'" lack of difference from norms of heterosexual culture, including citizenship, marriage, monogamy, two-parent households, "respectability," etc., a status unattainable and likely undesirable to a non-binary Palestinian, or a Black drag queen.

To round up our definitions of terms necessary for this discussion, homonationalism is the alignment of normative homosexuality, or homonormativity, with the values of patriotism, nationalism, and empire. One of its simplest illustrations would be gay soldiers serving in the US occupation army in Iraq, where the sexual torture by American troops of Iraqi prisoners in Abu Ghraib hinged on the American soldiers' and the mainstream USA's homophobia. When it comes to homonationalism, reactionaries, conservatives, and homonormative liberals alike have tended to accept Israel's propaganda as a gay-friendly country, whereas radical queers have not only exposed it, but they also present an alternative. And just as Black solidarity with Palestine is now becoming more visible, even though it is not a twenty-first-century phenomenon, so the queer uprising against empire, and colonialism, also pre-dates the recent denunciation of pinkwashing. The revolutionary Black intellectual and civil rights activist James Baldwin, for example, was denouncing the tyranny of sexual norms as early as the 1960s, and openly defied patriotism and imperialism, as he identified with dias-poric communities in France. Despite his prominent and significant role in the US Civil Rights movement, Baldwin had been shunned from the inner circle of Martin Luther King, Jr. because of his sexual-ity. In Paris, where he first lived before moving to the south of France, Baldwin had early on become intimately familiar with anti-Arab racism through his many interactions with Algerians. There he also developed and articulated his anti-imperialist stances, criticizing French imperial-ism in Vietnam and Algeria, while embracing the Black Panthers' view of Israel as a settler colonial country. In a 1979 article published in *The Nation* magazine, Baldwin writes:

> But the state of Israel was not created for the salvation of the Jews; it was created for the salvation of the Western interests. This is what is becoming clear (I must say that it was always clear to me). The Pal-estinians have been paying for the British colonial policy of "divide and rule" and for Europe's guilty Christian conscience for more than thirty years. Finally: there is absolutely—repeat: *absolutely*—no hope of establishing peace in what Europe so arrogantly calls the Middle East (how in the world would Europe know? having so dismally failed to find a passage to India) without dealing with the Palestinians.[38]

Baldwin did not so much proffer "solidarity" with the Palestinian cause, as much as it was "always clear" to him that the Palestinians, Algerians, and other "misérables" with whom he identified are all oppressed by the same system, Western imperialism, with its attention to "Western interests."

Decades later, INCITE! Women of Color Against Violence was one of the early US-based national feminists of color groups that denounced Israel's state-sanctioned gendered violence against all Palestinians, including gay and lesbian Palestinians. Shortly after forming in 2000, INCITE! published their "Palestine Points of Unity," which included support for the Palestinian liberation struggle, explaining that:

INCITE! condemns the violence directed at Palestinian women and communities, including rape, torture, imprisonment, destruction of homes, and the intentional maiming and murder of children in cold blood. INCITE! condemns the "Israeli" military's direct targeting of pregnant women at checkpoints ... INCITE! also condemns "Israel's" colonial and racist violence because it gives rise to domestic violence and sexual assault within Palestinian communities. We stand in solidarity with Palestinian women's resistance and we support their struggle for a self-determined liberation.[39]

INCITE! endorsed the Palestinian call for BDS shortly after it was first issued, also grounding its support in rejection of Israel's gendered violence against women, children, men, and its pinkwashing campaign which "projects [Israel]as a gay haven while barring Palestinian queers from joining gay parades."[40] At the same time as INCITE! was committing to supporting the Palestinian cause, it was engaging in its own campaigns against law enforcement violence against communities of color, especially women and trans people of color, here in the USA. The largest multiracial grassroots feminist collective in the USA, INCITE!'s membership, including membership in its national steering collective, numbered many Palestinians confronting American abuses. Its 2008 fact sheet, "Khaki and Blue: A Killer Combination," was one of the earliest denunciations of the joint trainings of US and Israeli forces, and looked at the devastating impacts of such trainings in the USA, where militarized police brutalized Black women in the aftermath of Hurricane Katrina in New Orleans, and US soldiers in Iraq were raping Iraqi men, women, and children, while supposedly on a mission to bring democracy to the country.[41]

Possibly the most elaborate anticolonial queer critique of the nexus of empire, homonormativity, and racism is that offered by Jasbir Puar. Giving the example of the Netherlands' "kiss test," which records reactions of newly arrived immigrants to the sight of two men kissing, Puar denounces the deeply seated racism of "advanced" countries that view the acceptance of homosexuality as a barometer of whether certain immigrant communities are acceptable to the nation state. Suspected homophobia is then used to continue the oppression of Brown, Black, and Muslim people, Puar explains. Therefore, pinkwashing is successful predominantly among liberals: they accept homonormativity, and condition their support of Palestinians, and other subjects of empire, upon these colonized cultures' acceptance of the "proper homo," the gay soldier at the service of empire. Puar's criticism, like that of many radical queers, is transnational, looking at state violence globally, by empire against communities of color.

Ultimately, the queer denunciation of pinkwashing and homonationalism hinges on the understanding that colonialism is a form of sexual violence, and cannot possibly empower those whose very lives, livelihoods, and lands it violates. It is a rejection of twenty-first-century-style colonialism, namely, white queers saving brown queers from their brown families. By exposing and denouncing pinkwashing and homonormativity, queers are also maintaining their own defiant rejection of binaries, borders, citizenship, and inclusion that can only ever come at the cost of the exclusion of others.

The Alternative is Already Here

The three examples we looked at above—the coming together of the criminalized Black and Brown communities against a hypermilitarized police engaged in urban warfare in metropolitan cities; the defiant indigeneity of the native peoples of Turtle Island, Hawaii, and Palestine; and the alliances between radical queers globally against homonormativity, pinkwashing, and the liberal gay white impulse to save brown queers from their own brown communities—are all manifestations of the anticolonial boomerang effect, or global intifada. What Palestine offers our allies today is an unsanitized contemporary manifestation of the violence of settler colonialism, yet one that also shines a light on this violence in other parts of the world. And our liberation struggles are enriched and revitalized by our coming together, not only on "reservations," such as Standing Rock, but throughout Turtle Island and the far reaches of US empire, just as the Indigenous people of this land are not only in solidarity with the refugees in Gaza, but with Palestinians throughout historic Palestine, and its diaspora. Similarly, the demand to abolish the police and end the carceral state, from the USA to Israel, and to consider all prisoners political prisoners, because of racialized criminalization, stems from the realization that, just as our enemy is united, so must our resistance be. And it is. There is no reversing the global intifada. Today, we are not "in solidarity" with Black, Indigenous, and queer groups, because one cannot be in solidarity with oneself: our communities are made up of Blacks, queer, Indigenous, immigrants, refugees, and Palestinians.

For over a century, ever since England promised part of Palestine to European Jews, the Palestinian people have wrestled with the challenge of obtaining national independence. The motivation was not a desire to have a state, as much as it was, and remains, the uncontainable need to be free. We have penned many documents and authored many books discussing the one-state solution. And we continue to produce visionary answers to the challenges facing us in our determination to live free from injustice. Today, even as an independent Palestinian statehood seems unrealistic, Palestinians are looking with optimism at decolonial possibilities that guarantee sovereignty and self-determination outside the confines of "statehood." The deep, irrepressible yearning for freedom and self-determination is what we have in common with the Indigenous people of Turtle Island, whose lands were stolen and traditions criminalized. We share it with Black Americans, who did not choose to come to this continent they have now been calling home for centuries. And we recognize it in queers who reject the expectations society imposes on their lives, that limit their exuberant creativity in return for inclusion. We have been through the same harrowing experiences of state violence, patriarchy, dispossession, incarceration; we have met in the belly of the beast and we are surfacing from its horrors together.

Epilogue:
Greater Than the Sum of
Our Parts

Black, Indigenous, Palestinian.
Immigrant, refugee, displaced, exiled.
Women, non-binary, gender non-conforming, improper homos,
queer.

Throughout this book, I have tried to emphasize the interconnectedness
of our struggles for freedom and self-determination. I have been intentional about de-exceptionalizing both Palestine and Israel. The Palestinians are the Indigenous people of the land of Palestine, and there are
Indigenous people throughout the globe. The Israelis are the colonizers, the settlers in that land and, sadly, there have historically been colonizers throughout the globe as well. The Palestinian experience is the
experience of the dispossessed and disenfranchised everywhere; the
"shared values" between Israel, the USA, and apartheid South Africa,
to name only the countries I have focused on here, are the values of the
European colonizer.

I have argued that the capacity to survive, even thrive, under the
harshest circumstances is a queer, feminist, abolitionist, intersectional, non-binary decolonial practice. It understands that reforming an
oppressive system—be it imperialism, settler colonialism, the police,
the military—only makes that system more effective, that is, more
oppressive. Today, a growing number of people are calling for the police
to be abolished, out of an understanding that policing as a system is not
broken, on the contrary it is doing exactly what it was always intended
to do. And while the idea of delegitimizing Zionist ideology altogether
may be novel to some, the Palestinians and our long-standing allies have

always understood that there can be no justice, no peace, under settler colonialism. To the arguments still being made today that "the current Israeli regime" is to blame, I have responded with rhetorical questions: when did Zionism, from Theodor Herzl's early writings to the current ethnic cleansing of Sheikh Jarrah and Masafer Yatta, not hinge on the dispossession of a pre-existing people? Which 1948 massacre or home demolition pales when compared to today's massacres? What aspect of al-Nakba, beginning in 1948, was not catastrophic for the Palestinians?

I know I have also raised many issues that I did not answer, and I would never claim to have all the answers. I have tried to delineate the many ways our many communities' paths have joined to form a web, a network of liberatory praxis, trusting that the dispossessed have the knowledge it takes to create a more just society where people are not only surviving, but where they are truly free. The voices of the elite, the "world leaders," the NGOs, have dominated the discourse about the oppressed for too long. Even when these are well-intentioned, they contribute to the erasure of the organic experience of the dispossessed: it is as if our knowledge is only valid when framed in the colonizer's language. This is racist gatekeeping. It is time to listen to the communities most impacted by the oppressive systems, because these are the communities that, overcoming misrepresentation, criminalization, and censorship, will lead the way to liberation.

To add insult to injury, we have been smeared for denouncing the injustice against us. The Indigenous who want their Land Back in Turtle Island are not labeled anti-white, nor were the Black Africans who rose to overthrow apartheid in South Africa accused of "reverse racism." And while Black Americans today are frequently subjected to the mean-spirited retort that "All Lives Matter," possibly the only unique aspect of the plight of the Palestinian people is the unparalleled weaponizing of the accusation of antisemitism as we denounce our oppression.

I sent this manuscript to my publisher a mere two days after the publication of the February 2022 Amnesty International report elaborating on Israel's apartheid regime which has oppressed Palestinians since 1948, the third such report in two years by an internationally respected NGO. That report itself would not have been possible without the work, over decades, of Palestinian human rights monitoring groups such as Al-Haq and Al Mezan, without the activism of countless individuals who put their bodies on the line, risking career and reputation, limb and life. But we have not only been denouncing our oppression, we have also crafted careful proposals for the alternative, always arguing that Palestine is indivisible and that, for justice to prevail, there can be only one state, from the river to the sea, free of patriarchy and heteronormativity.

We have no option but to persevere. We are the battered communities who did not capitulate. The women who were raped and survived to support and love our sisters. The youth who laugh at patriarchy, dismantling its institutions as they rise above its archaic binaries. And yes, the little boys who hurl rocks at tanks, because those small rocks contain their irrepressible yearning for an end to crushing oppression, an impulse so powerful it would poison them from within, if they do not catapult it out. It is a sad warped world indeed where anyone looking at a dispossessed child standing up to the invading occupier's assault tank views the child rather than the soldier driving the tank as a terrorist. We are the prisoners who dug their way to freedom with a rusted spoon, to inspire all prisoners everywhere: the underground, our soil, will free us. The foragers who sustain us with freshly gathered herbs, the peasants who know that reversing climate change is feminist, intersectional, decolonial, and the only way we can stay alive.

The tide has shifted. The year 2005 saw Palestinian civil society's call for Boycott, Divestment, and Sanctions gain global traction, as justice-minded people everywhere seized this opportunity to enact their solidarity with the Palestinian people. And if the decade of the 2010s is to be known as the decade of the Arab Springs and the "Palestine to Ferguson" rallies, the 2020s will likely be known as the decade when the deep connections among the wretched of the earth are cemented in joint analysis, practice, and engagement with decolonial struggle, the questioning of the possibility of the modern concept of militarized statehood to provide for collective rights.

Just as we have known, all along, that Zionism is racism, that Israel, the Jewish state, is not democratic, so we have also known that Palestine is indivisible. Not only is the two-state solution not feasible, but we must rise above all partitions, all boundaries. Decolonial vistas lift us away from the failed notion of the ethnonationalist state. Palestine is more than its fragments. And it is grassroots Palestinians, not politicians beholden to the archaic notion of borders enforced through violence, who have been proposing the alternative for decades.

Like abolitionists everywhere, we are busily thinking, organizing, dreaming, beyond the dystopic present. In the meantime, let us sustain ourselves with olives from trees as ancient as Palestine itself, and corn lovingly picked by hands the color of soil, not harvested through giant mechanical arms. Let us wash down this nutritious fare with fresh clean water, as we appreciate that, from Rafah to Standing Rock, Mni Wiconi, and the land is ours to care for, as it cares for us. We are coming together, beyond boundaries, and together, we are greater than the sum of our parts.

Appendix

Pledge—Palestine is a Feminist Issue

This Women's History Month, we, the undersigned, join the Palestinian Feminist Collective (PFC), a US based network of Palestinian and Arab women and feminists, in affirming Palestine as a feminist issue. Alongside the PFC, we build upon the history of Palestinian women and their co-strugglers who have worked to end multiple forms of oppression. We reject all appropriations of feminist and queer rights discourses that are used to dehumanize Palestinians, justify ongoing Zionist settler colonization of their homeland, and repress their political activism. In doing so, we commit to resisting gendered and sexual violence, settler colonialism, capitalist exploitation, land degradation and oppression in Palestine, on Turtle Island, and globally.

For decades, Palestinian feminists have resisted Israel's masculinist and militarized siege of Palestinian land and life. Since its inception, the Zionist settler colonial project has hinged on the expulsion of Palestinians from their homes and land, creating generations of landless Palestinian refugees. Zionist violence continues to dominate Palestinian lives in intimate ways. Throughout the homeland, Israel demolishes Palestinian homes, subjects Palestinian prisoners of conscience to systematic sexual and physical abuse and torture, and polices Palestinian bodies, sexualities, reproductive rights, and family life. Palestinians continue to affirm life in the face of the enduring *Nakba* (catastrophe), which takes place through deadly closure in the Gaza Strip, military occupation in the West Bank, legal designations of second-class citizenship in the settler state, exile in refugee camps and across the *shatat* (global diaspora), and denial of the right to return home.

We uphold the legacies of solidarity between Palestinian, Black, Indigenous, Third World feminist, working class, and queer communities who have struggled side-by-side within larger anti-colonial, anti-capitalist, and anti-racist movements in the US and globally. This stands in contrast to liberal feminist traditions in the US that continue to weaponize feminist discourses against Palestinians and other marginalized communities by failing to confront the structural forms of gendered and sexual violence inherent to settler/colonialism, imperialist wars, racial capitalism, and global white supremacy. Liberal and Zionist feminisms rely on Orientalist discourses to silence and undermine the collective aspirations of Palestinian women and their co-strugglers, contributing to intensified political repression that criminalizes free speech on Palestine and Palestinian liberation.

In the interest of advancing a truly intersectional and decolonial feminist vision for the United States, Palestine and our world, we hereby pledge to:

1. Embrace and advocate for Palestinian liberation as a critical feminist issue;
2. Support Palestinian rights to free speech and political organizing everywhere;
3. Reject the conflation of anti-Zionism with anti-Semitism, in particular the legal enforcement of the International Holocaust Remembrance Alliance's (IHRA) definition of anti-Semitism;
4. Heed the call of Palestinian civil society for Boycott, Divestment, and Sanctions;
5. Divest from militarism and invest in justice and community needs on Turtle Island;
6. Call for an end to US political, military, and economic support to Israel, and to all military, security, and policing collaborations.

Our commitment to the liberation of Palestinian lands and people is rooted in love, which is at the heart of all projects of decolonization. Our values grow out of embodied cultural wisdom and justice to transform our communities. We are committed to ending the greed, domination, and fragmentation so deeply entrenched in capitalism, colonial extraction, and US empire. We are re-imagining and re-creating a world free from systems of gendered, racial and economic exploitation that commodify human life and land. Ours is a vision for a radically different future based on life-affirming interconnectedness, empowering the working classes, and love for each other, land, life and the planet itself. For these reasons, **we pledge, today and everyday, to recognize Palestine as a Feminist Issue** and to uphold this commitment in our daily lives and organizing praxis.

To sign: https://actionnetwork.org/petitions/pledge-declaring-palestine-is-a-feminist-issue.

Notes

Preface

1. From a poem by Warsan Shire, "Home," Amnesty International, June 2016, www.amnesty.ie/wp-content/uploads/2016/06/home-by-warsan-shire.pdf.
2. I have in mind such iconic moments as when Micheline Awad took off her yellow heels to hurl a rock at an Israeli tank in Beit Sahour during the First Intifada, or Edward Said tossing a rock from Kafr Kila in southern Lebanon toward the Israeli border in 2000.
3. Nick Estes, "The Liberation of Palestine Represents an Alternative Path for Native Nations," *The Red Nation*, September 7, 2019, https://therednation.org/the-liberation-of-palestine-represents-an-alternative-path-for-native-nations/.

Introduction

1. Samir Abed-Rabbo, *ODS: The Case for One Democratic State in Historic Palestine*, Exeter: Center for Advanced International Studies, 2014, ii.
2. The November 2, 1917 Balfour Declaration, from Lord Balfour to Lord Rothschild, reads:

   > His Majesty's Government view with favour the establishment in Palestine of a national home for the Jewish people, and will use their best endeavours to facilitate the achievement of this object, it being clearly understood that nothing shall be done which may prejudice the civil and religious rights of existing non-Jewish communities in Palestine, or the rights and political status enjoyed by Jews in any other country.

3. Edward Said, *Culture and Imperialism*, New York: Vintage, 1994.
4. Many of the crimes committed in the context of colonialism, for example, "deportation or forcible transfer of population" and systemic "persecution against any identifiable group on political, racial, national, ethnic" grounds are considered crimes against humanity, but colonialism itself is not named—apartheid is.
5. The United Nations General Assembly first officially recognized apartheid as a crime against humanity in 1973. This designation was reaffirmed

in the 2002 Rome Statute of the International Criminal Court. Of course, as many have pointed, a belated recognition does not negate the crime before it was designated as such.

6. Human Rights Watch, "A Threshold Crossed: Israeli Authorities and the Crimes of Apartheid and Persecution," April 27, 2021, www.hrw.org/report/2021/04/27/threshold-crossed/israeli-authorities-and-crimes-apartheid-and-persecution.

7. B'Tselem: The Israeli Information Center for Human Rights in the Occupied Territories, "A Regime of Jewish Supremacy from the Jordan River to the Mediterranean Sea: This is Apartheid," January 2021, www.btselem.org/publications/fulltext/202101_this_is_apartheid.

8. Amnesty International, "Israel's Apartheid Against Palestinians: Cruel System of Domination and Crime Against Humanity," February 1, 2022, www.amnestyusa.org/wp-content/uploads/2022/01/Full-Report.pdf.

9. Palestinians have a unique, "hereditary" refugee status passed down from one generation to another, so long as a parent became a United Nations registered refugee during al-Nakba. UNRWA, the United Nations Relief and Work Agency for Palestinian Refugees in the Middle East, currently provides assistance to over 5.5 million Palestinian refugees, primarily in Palestine, Lebanon, Jordan, and Syria.

10. See, for example, Ben White's *Israeli Apartheid: A Beginner's Guide*, London: Pluto Press, 2009; Mats Svensson's *Crimes, Victims and Witnesses: Apartheid in Palestine*, Johannesburg: Real African Publishers, 2012; and Josh Ruebner's *Israel: Democracy or Apartheid State?* Northampton, MA: Olive Branch Press, 2017. And, most recently, B'Tselem's report, titled "This is Apartheid: The Israeli Regime Promotes and Perpetuates Jewish Supremacy Between the Mediterranean Sea and the Jordan River," 12 January 2021, www.btselem.org/press_releases/20210112_this_is_apartheid.

11. Patrick Wolfe, "Settler Colonialism and the Elimination of the Native," *Journal of Genocide Research* 8, no. 4 (2006): 387–409, https://doi.org/10.1080/14623520601056240.

12. Ibid., 388.

13. UNICEF report, "Health and Nutrition: State of Palestine," www.unicef.org/sop/what-we-do/health-and-nutrition.

14. See Or Kashti, "Israeli Professor's 'Rape as Deterrent' Statement Draws Ire," *Haaretz*, July 22, 2014, www.haaretz.com/.premium-prof-s-words-on-stopping-terror-draws-ire-1.5256331.

15. Ishaan Tharoor, "Israel's New Justice Minister Considers all Palestinian to be 'The Enemy,'" *The Washington Post*, May 7, 2015, www.washingtonpost.com/news/worldviews/wp/2015/05/07/israels-new-justice-minister-considers-all-palestinians-to-be-the-enemy/.

16. Human Rights Watch, "A Question of Security: Violence Against Palestinian Women and Girls," 18, no. 7(E) (November 2006), www.hrw.org/sites/default/files/reports/opt1106webwcover_0.pdf.

17. Nour Joudah, Intervention: "Gaza as Site and Method: The Settler Colonial City Without Settlers", *Antipode Online*, 24 August 2020, https://antipodeonline.org/2020/08/24/gaza-as-site-and-method/.

18. The Combahee River Collective Statement," https://americanstudies. yale.edu/sites/default/files/files/Keyword%20Coalition_Readings.pdf.

19. "Tal'at" is a Palestinian grassroots collective which denounces femicide within Palestinian society while arguing that national aspirations must be achieved through a feminist revolution. See https://palestinianyouth movement.com/no-free-homeland-without-free-women.

20. See my discussion of women's active participation in anticolonial resistance in Nada Elia, "Multiple Jeopardy: Gender and Liberation in Palestine," in *Palestine: A Socialist Introduction*, ed. Sumaya Awad and brian bean, Chicago, IL: Haymarket, 2020, 157–167.

21. See, for example, the excellent documentary *Naila and the Uprising*, directed by Julia Basha, Just Vision, 2018.

22. Mariame Kaba, "Yes, We Mean Literally Abolish the Police, Because Reform Won't Happen," *New York Times*, June 12, 2020.

23. Angela Davis, *Are Prisons Obsolete?* New York: Seven Stories Press, 2003, 107–108.

24. Red Nation statement, "The Liberation of Palestine Represents an Alternative Path for Native Nations," adopted in September 2019, https://therednation.org/the-liberation-of-palestine-represents-an-alternative-path-for-native-nations/.

Chapter 1

1. While this particular verbiage no longer appears online, The Israel Land Fund continues to offer help in what it calls "Land Acquisition and Reclamation." See, for example, www.israellandfund.com/acquisition-and-acquiring-land.

2. David Mark, "Sheikh Jarrah, Silwan, and the Need for Historical Justice," *Ateret Cohanim*, June 2, 2021, www.ateretcohanim.org/sheikh-jarrah-silwan-and-the-need-for-historical-justice/.

3. "My Grandmother, Icon of Palestinian Resistance," *The Nation*, July 20, 2020, www.thenation.com/article/world/palestinian-grandmother-resistance/.

4. Ibid.

5. See, for example, Akram Salhab and Dahoud al-Ghoul, "Jerusalem Youth at the Forefront of 2021's Unity Intifada," in *MERIP* (Middle East

Research and Information Project), October 11, 2021, https://merip.
org/2021/11/jerusalem-youth-at-the-forefront-of-2021s-unity-intifada/.

6. While terms such as "Indigenous," "native," and "aboriginal" are themselves
the consequence of colonialism—as no people thought of themselves as
"native" prior to conquest by outsiders—I mobilize them throughout this
book, and in my work elsewhere, as terms embraced by the colonized
people to discuss land-related struggles against colonialism and cultural
erasure.

7. "Richard Spencer Tells Israelis They 'Should Respect' Him: 'I'm a White
Zionist,'" *Haaretz*, August 16, 2017, www.haaretz.com/israel-news/
richard-spencer-to-israelis-i-m-a-white-zionist-resp.ect-me-1.5443480.

8. While the claim that all Ashkenazi Jews are descended from the Jewish
Kazars has been totally debunked, there is no controversy around the fact
that there are Jewish Kazars, who must have converted to Judaism at some
point; see the Zionist Jewish Virtual Library: www.jewishvirtuallibrary.
org/khazars.

9. Patrick Wolfe, "Settler Colonialism and the Elimination of the
Native," *Journal of Genocide Research* 8, nc. 4 (2006): 388, https://doi.
org/10.1080/14623520601056240.

10. Ibid.

11. In 1895, Theodor Herzl wrote in his diary that: "we shall try to spirt the
penniless population across the border .. Both the process of expropriation and the removal of the poor must be carried out discreetly and
circumspectly."

12. "Native Lives Matter," report by the Lakota People's Law Project,
February 2015, https://s3-us-west-1.amazonaws.com/lakota-peoples-
law/uploads/Native-Lives-Matter-PDF.pdf.

13. Amy Kaplan, *Our American Israel: The Story of an Entangled Alliance*, Cambridge, MA: Harvard University Press, 2018.

14. Cited in Kaplan, *Our American Israel*, 21.

15. Ibid., 75.

16. Ibid., 75.

17. Even though most studios during the Golden Age of Hollywood were
run by Jewish Americans, the majority of Jewish actors hid their Jewish
identity, and changed their names to less marked European ones. Paul
Newman's role in *Exodus* coincides with the beginnings of Jewish actors
making their cultural identity a mark of their screen identity, as is now
taken for granted thanks to the likes of Woody Allen, Jerry Seinfeld, and
Amy Schumer, to name but a very few.

18. In his 1919 essay, "Politics as a Vocation," Max Weber argues that a defining characteristic of a state is its claim to the exclusive right to use physical force, which he referred to as a "monopoly on violence."

19. *Al-Ahram Weekly*, August 30–September 5, 2001, no. 549:

    The most disturbing thing is that hardly any of the questioned Americans knew anything at all about the Palestinian story, nothing about 1948, nothing at all about Israel's illegal 34-year military occupation. The main narrative model that dominates American thinking still seems to be Leon Uris's 1950 novel *Exodus*.

20. The 2006 documentary, directed by Sut Jhally, is based on the 2001 book by the same title by Jack Shaheen, *Reel Bad Arabs: How Hollywood Vilifies a People*, New York: Olive Branch Press.

21. Oz Almog, *The Sabra: The Creation of the New Jew*, trans. Haim Watzman, Berkeley, CA: University of California Press, 2000.

22. Specific responses to gendered aspects of the struggle will be discussed in greater detail in Chapter 3, "Social and Political Liberation."

23. Ze'ev Jabotinsky, "The Iron Wall," original in Russian, April 11, 1923, Jabotinsky Institute, http://en.jabotinsky.org/media/9747/the-iron-wall.pdf.

24. Ibid.

25. Nikita Lalwani and Sam Winter-Levy, "Catholics Like the European Union More Than Protestants Do. This is Why," *Washington Post*, January 12, 2017, www.washingtonpost.com/news/monkey-cage/wp/2017/01/12/protestants-dont-like-the-european-union-compared-to-catholics-this-is-why/.

26. Jabotinsky, "The Iron Wall."

27. Ze'ev Jabotinsky, "The Ethics of the Iron Wall," 201/1923, www.infocenters.co.il/jabo/jabo_multimedia/articlesl/201_1923/אנגלית.pdf.

28. Ibid. British spelling appears in the translation (from the original Russian) that I am using here.

29. Jabotinsky, "The Ethics of the Iron Wall."

30. Ibid.

31. Sherene Seikaly, "The History of Israel/Palestine," in *Understanding and Teaching the Modern Middle East*, ed. Omnia El Shakry, Madison, WI: University of Wisconsin Press, 2018.

32. See, for example, Walid Khalidi, *All That Remains: The Palestinian Villages Occupied and Depopulated by Israel in 1948*, Washington, DC: Institute for Palestine Studies, 2006.

33. Golda Meir interview in *The Sunday Times*, June 15, 1969. Quoted in "A Talk with Golda Meir," *New York Times*, August 27, 1972, www.nytimes.com/1972/08/27/archives/a-talk-with-golda-meir.html.

34. "A Talk with Golda Meir."

35. Ibid.
36. Letty Cottin Pogrebin, "Golda Meir: May 3, 1898–December 8, 1978," *The Shalvi/Hyman Encyclopedia of Jewish Women,* https://jwa.org/encyclopedia/article/meir-golda. Last accessed September 12, 2021.
37. Quoted in Edward Said, *The Question of Palestine,* New York: Vintage, 1979, 14.
38. The statement is quoted in Ari Shavit, "An interview with Benny Morris," *Counterpunch,* January 16, 2004, www.counterpunch.org/2004/01/16/an-interview-with-benny-morris/. The interview is truly eye-opening, even damning, as it reveals the unmitigated racism of an Israeli public intellectual who claims to be "left wing."
39. Ibid.
40. Ibid.
41. Ibid.
42. Ibid.
43. Transcription of part of a talk given by Jeffrey Goldberg, editor-in-chief of *The Atlantic,* at the Jewish Community Center in New York City on December 6, 2019, YouTube, https://youtu be/TBgxez09_zk.
44. "A Jailer's Tale," Jeffery Goldberg interviewed by Blake Eskin in the *New Yorker,* September 25, 2006, available at: http://web.archive.org/web/20061027224457/http://www.newyorker.com/online/content/articles/061002on_onlineonly01.
45. We will have a more in-depth discussion of pinkwashing in Chapter 3 on "Social and Political Liberation."
46. Hen Mazzig, "OpEd: No, Israel Isn't a Country of Privileged and Powerful White Europeans," *Los Angeles Times,* May 20, 2019, www.latimes.com/opinion/op-ed/la-oe-mazzig-mizrahi-jews-israel-20190520-story.html.

Chapter 2

1. See, for example, Loubna Qutami, "Moving Beyond the Apartheid Analogy in Palestine and South Africa," *MERIP,* February 3, 2020, https://merip.org/2020/02/moving-beyond-the-apartheid-analogy-in-palestine-and-south-africa-trump/.
2. Raef Zreik, "Palestine, South Africa, and the Rights Discourse," *Journal of Palestine Studies* 34, no. 1 (Autumn 2004): 70, https://doi.org/10.1525/jps.2004.34.1.68.
3. Ibid.
4. See, for example, Noura Erakat, "What Role for Law in the Palestinian Struggle for Liberation?" Al-Shabaka briefs, March 4, 2014, https://al-shabaka.org/briefs/what-role-law-palestinian-struggle-liberation/; as

well as Noura Erakat's book, *Justice for Some: Law and the Question of Palestine*, Stanford, CA: Stanford University Press, 2020.

5. Erakat, "What Role for Law in the Palestinian Struggle for Liberation?"
6. Eve Tuck and K. Wayne Yang, "Decolonization is not a Metaphor," *Decolonization: Indigeneity, Education & Society* 1, no. 1 (2012): 1–40.
7. Idid., 25.
8. Ibid., 27.
9. Qutami, "Moving Beyond the Apartheid Analogy."
10. Valeria Minisini, "South Africa's Secondary Pandemic: A Crisis of Gender Based Violence," *Global Risk Insights*, March 28, 2021, https://globalriskinsights.com/2021/03/south-africas-secondary-pandemic-a-crisis-of-gender-based-violence/.
11. "Gender-Based Violence in South Africa," a report by SaferSpaces, Working Together for a Safer South Africa, www.saferspaces.org.za/understand/entry/gender-based-violence-in-south-africa.
12. "Gini Coefficient by Country 2021," online at: https://worldpopulation review.com/country-rankings/gini-coefficient-by-country.
13. Qutami, "Moving Beyond the Apartheid Analogy."
14. Aryn Baker, "What South Africa Can Teach Us as Worldwide Inequality Grows," *Time*, May 2, 2019, https://time.com/longform/south-africa-unequal-country/.
15. United Nations International Convention on the Suppression and Punishment of the Crime of Apartheid, www.un.org/en/genocideprevention/documents/atrocity-crimes/Doc.10_International%20Convention%20on%20the%20Suppression%20and%20Punishment%20of%20the%20Crime%20of%20Apartheid.pdf.
16. International Convention on the Elimination of All Forms of Racial Discrimination, adopted by UN General Assembly resolution 2106 (XX) on 21 December 1965, at: www.ohchr.org/en/instruments-mechanisms/instruments/international-convention-elimination-all-forms-racial.
17. The Rome Statute of International Criminal Law, adopted on 17 July 1998, in force on 1 July 2002, United Nations, Treaty Series, vol. 2187, no. 38544, Depositary: Secretary-General of the United Nations, www.icc-cpi.int/sites/default/files/RS-Eng.pdf.
18. Shira Robinson, *Citizen Strangers: Palestinians and the Birth of Israel's Liberal Settler State*, Stanford, CA: Stanford University Press, 2013.
19. Jennifer Davis interviewed by William Minter, Washington, DC, December 12, 2004, for *No Easy Victories: African Liberation and American Activists Over a Half Century, 1950–2000*, ed. William Minter, Gail Hovey, and Charles Cobb Jr., Trenton, NJ: Africa World Press, 2007, www.noeasyvictories.org/interviews/into9_davis.php.

20. Ibid.

21. Ibid.

22. Andrew Ross, *Stone Men: The Palestinians who Built Israel*, New York: Verso, 2019.

23. Ramzy Baroud, *My Father Was a Freedom Fighter: Gaza's Untold Story*, London: Pluto Press, 2010, 87.

24. Foreign Workers Law, Law #5751-1991; for details on the Foreign Workers Law, see International Labour Organization website, at: www.ilo. org/dyn/natlex/natlex4.detail?p_lang=en&p_isn=36145.

25. Cited in Michael Ellman and Smain Laacher, "Migrant Workers in Israel: A Contemporary Form of Slavery," a report commissioned by the Euro-Mediterranean Human Rights Network and the International Federation for Human Rights, www.fidh.org/IMG/pdf/il1806a.pdf.

26. Israel Drori, *Foreign Workers in Israel: Global Perspectives*, Albany, NY: SUNY Press, 2009.

27. See "ILO: Unemployment in the Occupied Palestinian Territory World's Highest," International Labour Organization, May 30, 2018, www.ilo. org/global/about-the-ilo/newsroom/news/WCMS_630876/lang--en/ index.htm; the Gisha report looking at women's unemployment, putting it at around 60 percent, see "Gaza Unemployment Rate Soars to 50.2% in Months Following May Escalation," *Gisha*, December 13, 2021, https:// gisha.org/en/gaza-unemployment-rate-soars-to-50-2-in-months-follow- ing-may-escalation/#:~:text=Unemployment%20among%20women%20 in%20Gaza%20also%20soared%20to,15%20or%20older%29%20 are%20counted%20in%20the%20workforce; another report put it at 90 percent!, see "Unemployment Among Gaza Women Hits Record High of 90%," *IMEMC News*, March 7, 2020, https://imemc.org/article/ unemployment-among-gaza-women-hits-record-high-of-90/.

28. "Khalifa Bin Zayed Al Nahyan Foundation Continues Supporting Iftar for Palestine Refugees in Gaza," press release, UNRWA, July 5, 2016, www.unrwa.org/newsroom/press-releases/khalifa-bin-zayed-al-nahyan- foundation-continues-supporting-iftar-palestine.

29. "Migrant Workers in Israel: A Contemporary Form of Slavery," International Federation for Human Rights, August 25, 2003, www.fidh. org/en/region/north-africa-middle-east/israel-palestine/Migrant- workers-in-Israel-A.

30. "The Law of Return," at www.nbn.org.il/life-in-israel/government- services/rights-and-benefits/the-law-of-return/.

31. Universal Declaration of Human Rights (1948) (UN 217A), United Nations, www.ohchr.org/en/resources/educators/human-rights- education-training/universal-declaration-human-rights-1948.

32. See UN Resolution 194, www.unrwa.org/content/resolution-194.
33. Uri Davis, *Israel: An Apartheid State*, London: Zed Books, 1987.
34. Ben White, *Israeli Apartheid: A Beginner's Guide*, London: Pluto Press, 2003.
35. An unofficial English translation of the Basic-Law: Israel—The Nation State of the Jewish People (Originally adopted in 5778-2018), including all the amendments adopted through May 1, 2022, can be found at: https://main.knesset.gov.il/EN/activity/Documents/BasicLawsPDF/BasicLawNationState.pdf.
36. 1958 Knesset Basic Law, https://m.knesset.gov.il/EN/activity/documents/BasicLawsPDF/BasicLawTheKnesset.pdf.
37. In early 2017, for example, Palestinian gunmen killed two Druze police officers in East Jerusalem. All those involved in the shooting, meaning the gunmen as well as the police officers, were Israeli citizens.
38. According to the Druze Veterans Association, www.druzevets.org.
39. Michele Chabin, "Arab in Israeli Knesset Sparks Outcry for Defending Palestinian Attacks," *USA Today*, February 19, 2016, www.usatoday.com/story/news/world/2016/02/19/arab-israel-knesset-controversy-palestinian-attacks-loyalty/80504122/.
40. Bel Trew, "Israel Passes Jewish Nation State Law Branded 'Racist' by Critics," *The Independent*, July 19, 2018, www.independent.co.uk/news/world/middle-east/israel-jewish-nation-state-law-passed-arabs-segregation-protests-benjamin-netanyahu-a8454196.html.
41. Ibid.
42. Adalah, "The Basic Law: Israel—The Nation State of the Jewish People," November 2018 report, www.adalah.org/uploads/uploads/Final_2_pager_on_the_JNSL_27.11.2018%20.pdf.
43. Anne-Marie Kriek, "South Africa Shouldn't Be Singled Out," *Christian Science Monitor*, October 12, 1989, archived at: www.csmonitor.com/1989/1012/ekri.html.
44. Ibid.
45. Ibid.
46. Ibid.
47. Ibid.
48. Ibid.

Chapter 3

1. Evelyn Shakir, *Bint Arab: Arab and Arab American Women in the United States*, Westport, CT: Praeger, 1997.

2. Cited in Nada Elia, "Multiple Jeopardy: Gender and Liberation in Palestine," in *Palestine: A Socialist Introduction*, ed. Sumaya Awad and brian bean, Chicago, IL: Haymarket, 2020.

3. "First Lady Hillary Rodham Clinton: Remarks for The United Nations Fourth World Conference on Women," Beijing, China, September 5, 1995, www.un.org/esa/gopher-data/conf/fwcw/conf/gov/950905175653.txt.

4. Ibid.

5. Layali Awwad, "Open Letter to Hillary Clinton from a Young Palestinian Feminist," *HuffPost* Contributor Platform, November 9, 2015, www.huffpost.com/entry/hillary-clinton-palestine_b_8513966.

6. Ibid.

7. INCITE! Women of Color Against Violence, https://incite-national.org/anti-militarism/.

8. Members of the Arab Women's Solidarity Association, "The Forgotten '-ism': An Arab American Women's Perspective on Zionism, Racism, and Sexism," in *The Color of Violence: The INCITE! Anthology*, ed. The INCITE! Women of Color Against Violence, Durham, NC: Duke University Press, 2006.

9. See, for example, the interview with Linda Sarsour following Emily Shire's OpEd in the *New York Times*: Collier Meyerson, "Can You Be a Zionist Feminist? Linda Sarsour Says No," *The Nation* March 13, 2017, www.thenation.com/article/archive/can-you-be-a-zionist-feminist-linda-sarsour-says-no/.

10. Mariam Barghouti, "No, You Can't be a Feminist and a Zionist," *The Forward*, November 27, 2017, https://forward.com/opinion/387675/no-you-cant-be-a-feminist-and-a-zionist/.

11. Ibid.

12. Gayatri Chakravorty Spivak, "Can the Subaltern Speak?" in *Marxism and the Interpretation of Culture*, ed. Cary Nelson and Lawrence Grossberg, London: Macmillan, 1988.

13. Lila Abu-Lughod, "Do Muslim Women Really Need Saving? Anthropological Reflections on Cultural Relativism and its Others," *American Anthropologist* 194, no. 3 (2002): 783–790; and Lila Abu-Lughod, *Do Muslim Women Need Saving?* Cambridge, MA: Harvard University Press, 2015.

14. Malek Alloula, *The Colonial Harem*, trans. Myrna Godzich and Wlad Godzich, Minneapolis, MN: University of Minnesota Press, 1986.

15. Ali Abuminah, "Israeli Lawmaker's Call for Genocide of Palestinians Gets Thousands of Facebook Likes," *The Electronic Intifada*, July 7, 2014, https://electronicintifada.net/blogs/ali-abunimah/israeli-lawmakers-call-genocide-palestinians-gets-thousands-facebook-likes.

16. Or Kashti, "Israeli Professor's 'Rape as Terror Deterrent' Statement Draws Ire," *Haaretz*, July 22, 2014, www.haaretz.com/.premium-prof-s-words-on-stopping-terror-draws-ire-1.5256331.

17. The Institute for Palestine Studies has published an Arabic translation of key passages of Ben-Gurion's Diary entries in 1947–1949, with passages that detail the rape of Palestinian women by Zionist militiamen; see *David Ben-Gurion, War Diaries (1947–1949)*, edited by Gershon Rivlin and Elhanan Orren, translated by Samir Jabbour, Washington, DC: Institute for Palestine Studies, 1998, www.palestine-studies.org/en/node/1648062.

18. Walid Khalidi, *Deir Yassin: Friday, 9 April, 1948*, Beirut: Institute for Palestine Studies, 1999.

19. Ari Shavit, "An Interview with Benny Morris," *Counterpunch*, January 16, 2004, www.counterpunch.org/2004/01/16/an-interview-with-benny-morris/.

20. Simona Sharoni, *Gender and the Israeli–Palestinian Conflict: The Politics of Women's Resistance*, Syracuse, NY: Syracuse University Press, 1995.

21. UN Human Rights Council annual report, February 1, 2008, "The Issue of Palestinian Pregnant Women Giving Birth at Israeli Checkpoints," https://documents-dds-ny.un.org/doc/UNDOC/GEN/G08/104/12/PDF/G0810412.pdf?OpenElement.

22. Rita Giacaman, Laura Wick, Hanan Abdul-Rahim, and Livia Wick, "The Politics of Childbirth in the Context of Conflict: Policies or de Facto Practices?" *Health Policy* 72, no. 2 (2005): 129–139, https://doi.org/10.1016/j.healthpol.2004.06.012. Available at: http://icph.birzeit.edu/system/files/childbrth%20policies%20in%20context%20of%20conflict%20Rita%20etc%202005.pdf.

23. Ibid., 133.

24. Ibid., 135.

25. Rhoda Ann Kanaaneh, *Birthing the Nation: Strategies of Palestinian Women in Israel*, Berkelely, CA: University of California Press, 2002, 62–63.

26. See, for example, "Any Palestinian is Exposed to Monitoring by the Israeli Big Brother," *The Guardian*, September 12, 2014, www.theguardian.com/world/2014/sep/12/israeli-intelligence-unit-testimonies.

27. Ibid.

28. Butina Kanaan Khoury's 2004 documentary, *Women in Struggle*, features a long segment on Odeh, where she tells of her rape during her interrogation.

29. Sabha al-Wawi, "My Daughter was Tortured and Forced to Spout Lies," *The National News*, (n.d.), www.thenationalnews.com/opinion/my-daughter-was-tortured-and-forced-to-spout-lies-1.143202/?utm_content=buffer40c52&fbclid=IwAR28APZquzWHAWAqIii12gDigEsiuEx3qZ4SJo1EeQ6Ds3VSf3pKY4hiMH4.

30. Ibid.
31. I use the term "queers" as an umbrella designation for LGBTQIA+ individuals for two reasons. One is that anytime one starts to list variations of sexualities, one is likely to run into the risk of exclusion by omission. Second is the fact that Palestinians use primarily two terms to respectfully refer to non-straight and/or non-cis individuals, one is *"mithali,"* which translates as same-sex, the other is "queer," a term which has made its way into the Arabic language.
32. Kimberlé W. Crenshaw, "Demarginalizing the Intersection of Race and Sex: A Black Feminist Critique of Antidiscrimination Doctrine, Feminist Theory and Antiracist Politics," *University of Chicago Legal Forum* 1989, no. 1, Article 8 (2015), http://chicagounbound.uchicago.edu/uclf/vol1989/iss1/8.
33. Deborah K. King, "Multiple Jeopardy, Multiple Consciousness: The Context of a Black Feminist Ideology," *Signs* 14, no. 1 (Autumn 1988): 42–72, https://doi.org/10.1086/494491.
34. Frances M. Beal, "Double Jeopardy: To Be Black and Female," *Meridians* 8, no. 2 (2008): 166–176, https://doi.org/10.2979/MER.2008.8.2.166. This article is a version of a speech Beal gave at the Third World Women's Alliance in New York, in 1969, titled "Black Women's Manifesto; Double Jeopardy: To Be Black and Female," available at: www.hartford-hwp.com/archives/45a/196.html. I put "power" in quotation marks because I question the appropriateness of this term as a descriptor of violence resulting from frustration.
35. Beal, "Double Jeopardy," 167.
36. I say "reportedly" because many scholars, including Nell Irvin Painter, who wrote *Sojourner Truth: A life, A Symbol,* have cast doubt on whether Sojourner Truth actually said these words. The question itself, though, was first recorded in the National Anti-Slavery Standard in 1863, and attributed to Truth.
37. Hillary Clinton's March 21, 2016 Speech at the AIPAC annual meeting, when she was running for election as US president. The transcript is available at *Time,* March 21, 2016: https://time.com/4265947/hillary-clinton-aipac-speech-transcript/.
38. The "Combahee River Collective Statement," first issued in April 1977, is available at *Black Past,* www.blackpast.org/african-american-history/combahee-river-collective-statement-1977/.
39. Ibid.
40. See, for example, Imara Jonez, "Confronting Black Men's Roles in the Murders of Black Transgender Women May Be the Only way to Save our Lives," *The Grio,* June 24, 2019, https://thegrio.com/2019/06/24/

confronting-black-mens-roles-in-the-murder-of-black-transgender-women/; and the video "Why are Black Men Killing Black Trans Women?" YouTube, August 30, 2020, https://youtu.be/c2LQXO2RXTM.

41. Beal, "Double Jeopardy," 169.

42. The US Bureau of Justice Statistics's 1999 report was one of the first national reports to include research on the race of perpetrators of sexual assault against Indigenous women, showing that most were white men; see Lawrence A. Greenfeld and Steven K. Smith, *American Indians and Crime*, Washington, DC: Bureau of Justice Statistics, 1999, https://bjs.ojp.gov/content/pub/pdf/aic.pdf. Numerous studies since that initial report confirm that sexual violence against Indigenous women differs from the pattern of intraracial sexual violence that characterizes other ethnic communities, with most Indigenous women experiencing assault and rape by white men. See also Lyndsey Gilpin, "Native American Women Still Have the Highest Rate of Rape and Assault," *High Country News*, June 7, 2016, www.hcn.org/articles/tribal-affairs-why-native-american-women-still-have-the-highest-rates-of-rape-and-assault.

43. Sarah Deer, *The Beginning and End of Rape: Confronting Sexual Violence in Native America*, Minneapolis, MN: University of Minnesota Press, 2015.

44. See, for example, "Violence from Extractive Industry 'Man Camps' Endangers Indigenous Women and Children," *First Peoples Worldwide*, University of Colorado, January 29, 2020, www.colorado.edu/program/fpw/2020/01/29/violence-extractive-industry-man-camps-endangers-indigenous-women-and-children.

45. The Red Nation, *The Red Deal: Indigenous Action to Save Our Earth*, New York: Common Notions, 2021, 99.

46. Ibid.

47. "Health and Nutrition," UNICEF: State of Palestine, www.unicef.org/sop/what-we-do/health-and-nutrition.

48. I personally favor the term "feminicide," which comes out of the Latin American context, and implicates the state and legal system in the normalization of the murder of women by, for example, accounting for "mitigating circumstances" in the legal discussion of these "crimes of passion." However, as the Palestinian feminist activists and researchers whose work I foreground use "femicide," I will use this term instead.

49. Nadera Shalhoub-Kevorkian, "Racism, Militarization and Policing: Police Reactions to Violence Against Palestinian Women in Israel," *Social Identities* 10 (2004): 171–193.

50. Nadera Shalhoub-Kevorkian and Suhad Daher-Nashif, "Femicide and Colonization: Between the Politics of Exclusion and the Culture of

Control," *Violence Against Women* 19, no. 3 (2013): 295–315, https://doi.org/10.1177/1077801213485548.

51. Ibid., 297.

52. Ibid., 311.

53. Suhad Daher-Nashif, "Intersectionality and Femicide: Palestinian Women's Experiences With the Murders of Their Beloved Female Relatives," *Violence Against Women* 28, no. 5 (2021): 1081, https://doi.org/10.1177/10778012211014561.

54. "PYM Celebrates International Women's Day 2020," Palestinian Youth Movement, March 8, 2020, https://palestinianyouthmovement.com/no-free-homeland-without-free-women; or "'No Free Homeland Without Free Women': Palestinian Youth Movement Celebrates International Women's Day 2020," *Mondoweiss*, March 8, 2020, https://mondoweiss.net/2020/03/no-free-homeland-without-free-women-palestinian-youth-movement-celebrates-international-womens-day-2020/.

55. "'No Free Homeland Without Free Women.'"

56. Ibid.

57. Hala Marshoud and Riya AlSanah, "Tal'at: A Feminist Movement that is Redefining Liberation and Reimagining Palestine," *Mondoweiss*, February 25, 2020, https://mondoweiss.net/2020/02/talat-a-feminist-movement-that-is-redefining-liberation-and-reimagining-palestine/.

58. The Palestinian Feminist Collective Pledge was published online, on the group's Facebook page, as well as on the online news sites *Mondoweiss* and *Jadaliyyah*. It is reproduced in its entirety in the Appendix.

59. See, for example, Nada Elia, "Israel–Palestine: How Subcontracting the Occupation Fuels Gendered Violence," *Middle East Eye*, July 2, 2021, www.middleeasteye.net/opinion/israel-palestine-subcontracting-occupation-gendered-violence-fuels.

60. "*isqat siyasi*" roughly translates as "political character assassination," "political slander," or "political defamation."

61. "Beyond Propaganda: Pinkwashing as Colonial Violence," *AlQaws*, October 18, 2020, www.alqaws.org/siteEn/print?id=86&type=1.

62. Some important sources on Pinkwashing include the USCPR's "Palestine as a Queer Struggle," *US Campaign for Palestinian Rights*, co-authored by Nada Elia, https://uscpr.org/queerstruggle; Jasbir Puar's "Israel's Gay War Propaganda," *The Guardian*, July 1, 2010, www.theguardian.com/commentisfree/2010/jul/01/israels-gay-propaganda-war; the documentary *Pinkwashing Exposed*, directed by Dean Spade, available for viewing at https://pinkwashingexposed.net; and Nada Elia's "Gay Rights with a Side of Apartheid," *Journal of Settler Colonial Studies* 2, no. 2 (2012): 49–68, https://doi.org/10.1080/2201473X.2012.10648841.

63. For "Brand Israel," see Israel21c, www.israel21c.org.
64. "The Chosen Ones: Israeli Defense Forces," *Maxim.com*, September 13, 2007, www.maxim.com/women/chosen-ones-israeli-defense-forces/.
65. Ethan Bonner, "After Gaza, Israel Grapples with Crisis of Isolation," *New York Times*, March 18, 2009, www.nytimes.com/2009/03/19/world/middleeast/19israel.html.
66. Mel Bezalel, "Gay Pride Used to Promote Israel Abroad," *Jerusalem Post*, June 7, 2009, www.jpost.com/israel/gay-pride-being-used-to-promote-israel-abroad.
67. Noa Meir, quoted in Bezalel, "Gay Pride Used to Promote Israel Abroad."
68. Puar, "Israel's Gay Propaganda War."
69. "Queer Liberation & Palestine," *AlQaws*, May 26, 2021, www.alqaws.org/articles/Queer-Liberation-Palestine?category_id=0.
70. Ibid.
71. Ghadir Shafie, "Pinkwashing: Israel's International Strategy and Internal Agenda," *Kohl: A Journal for Body and Gender Research* 1, no. 1 (Summer 2015): 82–86, https://kohljournal.press/pinkwashing-israels-international-strategy.
72. See, for example, Sarah Schulman, *Israel/Palestine and the Queer International*, Durham, NC: Duke University Press, 2012; Elia, "Gay Rights with a Side of Apartheid"; and USCPR with Elia, "Palestine as a Queer Liberation Struggle."
73. Shafie, "Pinkwashing," 83.
74. Ibid., 84.
75. Ibid., 84.
76. Ibid., 85.
77. The names of the queer Palestinians featured in this documentary have been modified to preserve their anonymity.
78. *The Invisible Men*, directed by Yariv Mozer, 2012.
79. Sigal Samuel, "The Invisible Men Accused of Pinkwashing," *The Daily Beast*, November 12, 2012, www.thedailybeast.com/the-invisible-men-accused-of-pinkwashing.
80. Mozer, *The Invisible Men*.
81. See my extant discussion of *Men of Israel* and other pinkwashing initiatives in Elia, "Gay Rights with a Side of Apartheid."
82. Rana Barakat, "Lifta, the Nakba, and the Museumification of Palestine's History," *NAIS: Journal of the Native American and Indigenous Studies Association* 5, no. 2 (Fall 2018): 5, muse.jhu.edu/article/721563.
83. Michael Lucas, *Men of Israel*, 2009, https://forward.com/culture/114183/pornographic-stimulus-plan/.

Chapter 4

1. Winona LaDuke, "'Columbus Day' Reminds Us Why the US Owes Reparations to Native People," *Truthout*, October 14, 2019, https://truthout. org/articles/columbus-day-reminds-us-why-the-us-owes-reparations-to-native-people/.

2. Aylin Woodward, "Climate Changed After Europeans killed 90% of Indigenous American," *Business Insider*, February 9, 2019, www. businessinsider.com/climate-changed-after-europeans-killed-indigenous-americans-2019-2.

3. Carolyn Merchant, *American Environmental History: An Introduction*, New York: Columbia University Press, 2007, 20.

4. Tim Stanley, "Teddy Roosevelt Laid Bare," *History Today* 63, no. 3 (2012), www.historytoday.com/archive/contrarian/teddy-roosevelt-laid-bare.

5. Hannah Seo, "Indigenous Harvest Rights Still Under Attack in the Upper Great Lakes," *Environmental Health News*, April 29, 2021, www. ehn.org/indigenous-harvest-rights-2652632895/troubling-trends-in-tribal-harassment.

6. Kay LaFonde, "Tribal Citizens Say Harassment Affects How They Hunt, Fish," *Michigan Radio*, May 30, 2019, www.michiganradio.org/ environment-science/2019-05-30/tribal-citizens-say-harassment-affects-how-they-hunt-fish.

7. For an excellent report about the tensions between settler environmentalists and the Shoshone nation, see Chris Clarke, "When Green Groups Fought Native Rights: The Timbisha Shoshone in Death Valley," *KCET*, January 2, 2017, www.kcet.org/shows/tending-the-wild/when-green-groups-fought-native-rights-the-timbisha-shoshone-in-death-valley.

8. See Alex Fox, "Sierra Club Grapples with Founder John Muir's Racism," *Smithsonian Magazine*, July 24, 2020, www.smithsonianmag.com/smart-news/sierra-club-grapples-founder-john-muirs-racism-180975404/.

9. Sarah Deer, *The Beginning and End of Rape: Confronting Sexual Violence in Native America*, Minneapolis, MN: University of Minnesota Press, 2015, 51.

10. Ibid.

11. "PFC Statement on the Criminalization of Palestinian NGOs," Palestinian Feminist Collective, Facebook, November 9, 2021, www.facebook.com/ palestinianfeministcollective/posts/292031239595458.

12. Diaries, June 12, 1895. For *The Complete Diaries of Theodor Herzl*, edited by Raphael Patai, translated by Harry Zohn, London: Herzl Press and New York: Thomas Yoselcff, 1960, see https://archive.

org/stream/TheCompleteDiariesOfTheodorHerzl_201606/
TheCompleteDiariesOfTheodorHerzlEngVolume1_OCR_djvu.txt.

13. Ibid.

14. Conal Urquhart, "Gaza on Brink of Implosion as Aid Cut-Off Starts to Bite," *The Guardian*, April 16, 2006, www.theguardian.com/world/2006/apr/16/israel.

15. An unofficial translation of the study was published by Gisha and is available at: www.gisha.org/UserFiles/File/publications/redlines/red-lines-presentation-eng.pdf.

16. For an overview of the water apartheid in Palestine, see Amnesty International's report, "The Occupation of Water," November 29, 2011, www.amnesty.org/en/latest/campaigns/2017/11/the-occupation-of-water/. Another report, Susan Koppelman and Zayneb Alshalalfeh, "The Human Right to Water in Palestine," for LifeSource, a Palestinian collective founded in 2007 and active through 2012, is available at: www.blueplanetproject.net/documents/RTW/RTW-Palestine-1.pdf.

17. For a brief overview, see Mersiha Gadzo "How Israel Engages in 'Water Apartheid,'" *Al-Jazeera*, October 21, 2017, www.aljazeera.com/news/2017/10/21/how-israel-engages-in-water-apartheid.

18. Melanie Lidman, "After Devastating Fires, the JNF Skips Trees for the Forest," *Times of Israel*, December 19, 2016, www.timesofisrael.com/after-devastating-fires-jnf-skips-trees-for-the-forest/.

19. Daniella Cheslow, "As More Israelis Go Vegan, Their Military Adjusts Its Menu," *NPR*, December 10, 2015, www.npr.org/sections/thesalt/2015/12/10/459212839/why-so-many-israeli-soldiers-are-going-vegan.

20. For a general discussion of the impact of climate change on Indigenous communities, I highly recommend the Minority Rights Group publication, "Minority and Indigenous Trends 2019: Focus on Climate Justice," June 26, 2019, https://minorityrights.org/publications/minority-and-indigenous-trends-2019/. I particularly appreciated its consistent reminder that all solutions should include "a particular focus on women, children, LGBTQ+ people, people with disabilities and other groups who face intersectional discrimination on account of their minority or indigenous identity."

21. Winona LaDuke, "'Columbus Day' Reminds Us Why the US Owes Reparations to Native People."

22. *The Path of Peasant and Popular Feminism in La Via Campesina*, 2021, https://viacampesina.org/en/publication-the-path-of-peasant-and-popular-feminism-in-la-via-campesina/.

23. Ibid., 14.

24. Ibid.

25. Raj Patel, "Food Sovereignty—A Brief Introduction," November 2, 2009, https://rajpatel.org/2009/11/02/food-sovereignty-a-brief-introduction/.

26. Ibid.

27. Michelene E. Pesantubbee, *Choctaw Women in a Chaotic World: The Clash of Cultures in the Colonial Southeast*, Albuquerque, NM: University of New Mexico Press, 2005.

28. Nicholas Mancall-Bitel, "Brit Reed is Leading a New Generation of Indigenous Chefs," *Bon Appétit*, May 18, 20:8, www.bonappetit.com/story/brit-reed.

29. Asmaa al-Ghoul, "Gaza Cancer Rates cn Rise," *Al Monitor*, March 29, 2013, www.al-monitor.com/originals/2013/03/cancer-rates-soar-gaza-war.html.

30. Laila M. El-Haddad, *The Gaza Kitchen: A Palestinian Culinary Journey*, illustrated by Maggie Schmitt, Charlottesville, VA: Just World Books, 2013.

31. Natifs, North American Traditional Indigenous Food Systems, www.natifs.org.

32. Nasser Jaber and Alex Hernandez, "Palestinian-Mexican Cooking Demonstration with Migrant Kitchen," January 13, 2021, Panel at Palestine Writes Literature Festival, at: www.facebook.com/watch/?v=438508887187310.

33. Reem Assil's restaurant, Reem's in Oakland, California, www.reemscalifornia.com/about.

34. Cited in Rima Najjar, "Life in Abu Dis Continues Quietly," *Biography* 37, no. 2 (Spring 2014): 637, https://doi.org/10.1353/bio.2014.0027.

35. The quote comes from Mahmoud Darwish's poem: "On This Land" see *The Butterfly's Burden: Poems by Mahmoud Darwish*, translated by Fady Joudah, Port Townsend, WA: Copper Canyon Press, 2007, 203.

Chapter 5

1. "Joe Biden Says if Israel Didn't Exist, the US Would Have to Invent One to Protect US Interests," YouTube, March 3, 2019, https://youtu.be/FYLNCcLfIkM.

2. "The Iron Wall," original in Russian, April 11, 1923, Jabotinsky Institute, http://en.jabotinsky.org/media/9747/the-iron-wall.pdf.

3. Ibid.

4. For an analysis of the militarization of US police forces as a result of their training with Israeli forces, see Nada Elia, "Kill Like an Israeli," *Mondoweiss*,

July 19, 2017, https://mondoweiss.net/2017/07/kill-like-an-israeli/; and Nada Elia, "Defund the Police: We Need an Alternative to the Racist US System," *Middle East Eye*, June 10, 2020, www.middleeasteye.net/opinion/defund-police-we-need-alternative-racist-us-system.

5. See "What is Krav Maga," Krav Maga Worldwide, https://kravmaga.com/what-is-krav-maga/.

6. Ibid.

7. "McKinney Officer Was No Rookie," *Dallas Morning News*, June 8, 2015. www.dallasnews.com/news/2015/06/09/mckinney-officer-was-no-rookie/.

8. See *The Color of Violence: The INCITE! Anthology*, ed. INCITE! Women of Color Against Violence, Durham, NC: Duke University Press, 2006; and *Law Enforcement Violence Against Women of Color & Trans People of Color: A Critical Intersection of Gender Violence & State Violence*, self-published, 2008, available at: https://incite-national.org/stop-law-enforcement-violence/.

9. Steven Salaita, *Inter/Nationalism: Decolonizing Native America and Palestine*, Minneapolis, MN: University of Minnesotta, 2016, 24.

10. "When I See Them, I See Us," YouTube, March 7, 2021, www.youtube.com/watch?v=F5RY4MjdoXM: "Featuring Ms. Lauryn Hill, Danny Glover, DAM, Omar Barghouti, Alice Walker, Angela Davis, Yousef Erakat, Annemarie Jacir, Boots Riley, Dr. Cornel West, and many others."

11. Cited in Nathan Thrall, "How the Battle Over BDS and Anti-Semitism is Fracturing American Politics," *New York Times*, March 28, 2019, www.nytimes.com/2019/03/28/magazine/battle-over-bds-israel-palestinians-antisemitism.html?comments.

12. Valerie Williams, "Mom Gives Birth at Standing Rock: 'Having Babies is My Act of Resistance,'" *Scary Mommy*, November 25, 2016, www.scarymommy.com/native-american-mom-gives-birth-at-standing-rock/.

13. Ibid.

14. Rima Najjar, "Life in Abu Dis Continues Quietly," *Biography* 37, no. 2 (Spring 2014): 637, https://doi.org/10.1353/bio.2014.0027.

15. "2015 Black Solidarity Statement with Palestine," *Black for Palestine*, www.blackforpalestine.com/read-the-statement.html.

16. Ibid.

17. "A Cut in US Military Expenditures and a Reallocation of those Funds to Invest in Domestic Infrastructure and Community Wellbeing," May 2020, *A Vision for Black Lives*, https://m4bl.org/wp-content/uploads/2020/05/CutMilitaryExpendituresOnePager.pdf.

18. Michael R. Fischbach, *Black Power and Palestine: Transnational Countries of Color*, Stanford, CA: Stanford University Press, 2018, 17.

19. Ibid., 19.
20. Quoted in Khury Petersen-Smith, "Ccps Here, Bombs There: Black–Palestinian Solidarity," in *Palestine: A Socialist Introduction*, ed. Sumaya Awad and brian bean, Chicago, IL: Haymarket, 2020, 173.
21. Suheir Hammad, *Born Palestinian, Born Black and The Gaza Suite*, Brooklyn, NY: UpSet Press, 2010.
22. Palestine Writes, Twitter: @PalestineWrites, December 6, 2020, https://twitter.com/palestinewrites/status/1335675757352407042.
23. Linda Sarsour, *We Are Not Here to be Bystanders: A Memoir of Love and Resistance*, New York: 37Ink, 2020, 39.
24. Ibid., 46.
25. Speech on the centenary of the US overthrow of Hawai'i, "We Are Not Americans", November 8, 2016, YouTube, https://youtu.be/SDsx1mUpiI4.
26. See Lila Abu-Lughod, "Imagining Palestine's Alter-Natives; Settler Colonialism and Museum Politics," *Critical Inquiry* 47, no. 1 (Autumn 2020), https://doi.org/10.1086/710906.
27. Samir Abed-Rabbo, *ODS: The Case for One Democratic State in Historic Palestine*, Exeter: Center for Advanced International Studies, 2014.
28. Mazin Qumsiyeh, *Sharing the Land of Canaan: Human Rights and the Israeli–Palestinian Struggle*, London: Pluto Press, 2004.
29. Ali Abunimah, *One Country: A Bold Proposal to End the Israeli-Palestinian Impasse*, New York: Picador, 2007.
30. Laila Farsakh, ed., *Rethinking Statehood in Palestine: Self-Determination and Decolonization Beyond Partition*, Oakland, CA: University of California Press, 2021.
31. The Red Nation, http://therednation.org/about/.
32. The Red Nation, *The Red Deal, Indigenous Actions to Save our Earth*, New York: Common Notions, 2021, 49.
33. Ibid., 63.
34. Ibid., 64.
35. Nelson Rolihlahla Mandela: 18 July 1918–5 December 2013, "Address by President Nelson Mandela at International Day of Solidarity with Palestinian People, Pretoria," 4 December 1997, www.mandela.gov.za/mandela_speeches/1997/971204_palestinian.htm.
36. Steven Salaita, "Inter/Nationalism: Decolonizing Native America and Palestine," *Rising Up with Sonali*, circa 2017, https://vimeo.com/193755150.
37. Jasbir K. Puar, *Terrorist Assemblages: Homonationalism in Queer Times*, Durham, NC: Duke University Press, 2017.
38. James Baldwin, "Open Letter to the Born Again," *The Nation*, September 29, 1970, www.thenation.com/article/archive/open-letter-born-again/.

39. "Palestine Points of Unity," INCITE!, https://incite-national.org/palestine-points-of-unity/.
40. "INCITE! Supports the Palestinian Call for BDS," https://incite-national.org/incite-palestinian-bds/.
41. While the toolkit, like many of INCITE!'s resources, does not name individual authors, I, a Palestinian woman, co-edited it with Andrea Ritchie, a Black organizer. I mention this in order to point out the contributions of Palestinians to American grassroots, radical feminist activism. See "Khaki and Blue: A Killer Combination: US Police Brutality Abroad," INCITE!, https://incite-national.org/khaki-and-blue-a-killer-combination/.

Index